*ISBN 80-900129-2-2*

# GOLEM

EDUARD
PETIŠKA

MARTIN

ברוך הנותן

ליעף כח

שמנגיניה

נכאו אומ ואין דרך

*TO THE MEMORY OF THE DEAD,*
*AND TO THE MEMORY OF THE LIVING*

The fog rises,
silent
and serene,
from
the Vltava . . .

It is December. The fog rises, silent and serene, from the Vltava. Its white clusters recede from the oldest ford in Prague. It enters the Old Town of Prague, the streets of the former ghetto, and the Old Jewish Cemetery. Nightfall follows in its murky footsteps.

The whitish gloom descends, silent and serene, on the ancient tombstones of the Jewish cemetery. They clasp each other. There are thousands of them. Who lies below them in the dense layers, who has rested here for centuries?

In the dusk we can see a Hebrew inscription and a symbol carved on a stone. Here a violin indicates the place where a musician is buried and there a pair of scissors suggests a tailor. A book-printer is immortalized by a book, a pharmacist by a mortar and pestle. The symbols of the Jewish clans and names slowly disappear in the dusk. Raised hands of the Cohanim are pointing to Heaven, lions remind us of the Hebrew name Jehudah, stags of the name Zebi. Stone roses still bloom above the tombs of Roses, and the scene of the paradise shows the place where Eve sleeps for ever. Stone grapes signify fertility and wisdom.

The tombstones made of rose Slivenec marble are dampened by the fog, and sometimes gleam, as if the reflection of the long-past diminishing fire quivered within them. Those who fled the fires of the Jewish Town together with those who fell victim to them, now rest deep beneath the earth. And with them the stories of their lives, their dreams and reality.

Butchers who were always weighed towards the end of the week and gave an equivalent weight of meat to the poor, sleep here, as well as the wise Cohen, who travelled to see the Pope with a request to absolve Emperor Ferdinand I from his vow to banish the Jews from his empire. Learned rabbis found peace here after years of seeking the truth, as did Jewish tradesmen travelling about on business all their lives, peddlers, goldmiths and physicians, poor carriers and rich people. Their past became a part of history and legends, though often without their names.

Behind the rows of the tombstones at the back of the churchyard people walk about, seeking among the tombs. They stop by the tombstone of the famous Jewish scholar, Rabbi Löw. Now they lean over the tombstone. Perhaps they lay a little stone there, to respect the memory of the dead. It is an old Jewish custom, from the time when the Jews were wandering in the desert, where there were no flowers. Perhaps they put also a note with their secret wishes into the cracks in the tombstone, wishing them to be fulfilled. Many centuries have not destroyed the faith in the rabbi's miraculous power.

Now the fog steps softly near the tomb of the famous rabbi. In a moment it will envelop all around. The tombstones are losing their contours. What is close becomes distant and what is distant becomes close.

The footsteps of the last visitor are growing quiet. Only silence and dusk enter. It is the hour when legends and tales come to visit those who like to listen.

Let us listen with them.

In the ancient and famous town of Worms, near the river Rhine in Germany, there lived, many centuries ago, a respected rabbi named Bezalel. The spring was approaching, and his wife was expecting a child. The Rhine murmured, as there was a thaw in the mountains. Jewish people prepared for the spring festival of Passover.

When the night of Passover fell, all Jewish families sat down to their tables, to celebrate the liberation of their ancestors from slavery in Egypt, in accordance with ancient tradition. On their festive tables everything had its place and purpose. Bitter herbs provided a memory of the bitter life in Egypt, grated apples recalled the clay from which Jews made bricks for the Egyptians, red wine reminded them of the pharaoh's cruelty when, punished by leprosy, he bathed in the blood of Jewish children, in order to recover. Salty water in a dish on the table was a reminder of the waves of the Red Sea, which had parted before the fleeing Jews, and closed up before their Egyptian persecutors. They ate unleavened bread, just as at that time when they were leaving Egypt in haste and there was no time for baking the bread leavened.

The windows were shining in the Jewish Town, festive candles burned on the tables, and through the walls of the houses the singing of the psalms was heard in the streets. The family of Rabbi Bezalel also celebrated Passover. In

*11*

the middle of this wonderful festive time the expectant mother was beset by pains. The servants of Bezalel's house ran out to fetch the midwife, who used to help women in labour in these difficult moments.

Just as the servants ran out into the street, a suspicious-looking man with a bag on his back was sneaking by. When he saw the people running towards him, he hurried away, as fast as he could. The night guard, going about the town, suspected that the man had stolen something and that the servants were pursuing him. They stopped him and began to untie his bag.

They discovered that he was carrying a dead man. The man maintained that he was not a murderer and told them who the actual murderers were. He was only supposed to bring the dead man to the Jewish Town, so that the Jews would be accused of the death of a Christian. There was a superstition spread among the common people that Jews need Christian blood for preparing their Passover breads. A dead Christian in the Jewish Town during Passover would have caused a dangerous commotion all over Worms. Therefore the Jews were glad when the guard took the man with the bag to prison.

That night Bezalel's wife gave birth to a boy. Everyone who knew the story of what had preceded his birth welcomed him with joy. The coming of the boy itself brought peace and quiet to the persecuted nation.

Over his son's cradle, honorable Rabbi Bezalel said:

"He was born to bring us consolation, to give us strength and comfort. At his birth a happy star was lit up. He will help us where help will seem impossible to the others. Let his name be Judah, since it is written: Judah is a young lion."

The baby lay in the cradle and appeared too tiny and delicate to be able to carry the fame and greatness that awaited him. And so they started to call him Judah, son of Bezalel, or Jehudah ben Bezalel.

## IN PRAGUE

Little Judah ben Bezalel was growing, but his spirit grew faster than his body. It was customary at that time for young Jews to look for wisdom in renowned schools abroad. One of the most famous Jewish schools was in Prague. Thus young Judah set out to the city. He thirsted after knowledge, and it seemed to him that Prague's well of learning was inexhaustible.

In Prague his mind opened into blossom. Everyone praised his diligence and sharpness of mind. Soon he was the first among his fellows.

In the Jewish Town of Prague there also lived a rich Jew named Samuel Shmelke.He had a son who lived in Poland, in the town of Przemyśl, honoured with respect and high reputation. Samuel also had a daughter. Her name was Perl, or Pearl. She was old enough to be engaged. Samuel was looking for a fiancé for her. His choice fell on young Judah, who soon became engaged to Perl, in accordance with the custom of that time. But after the engagement Samuel sent Judah to stay with his son in Poland, and the engaged couple had to part. Perl stayed in Prague with her father, while Judah travelled throughout Poland and made the acquaintance of scholars in Poland's Jewish schools.

Young Judah entered the ever-increasing world of wisdom, but the golden light of Samuel's wealth diminished. The Jewish Town was affected by cruel taxes. Samuel's trade deteriorated, and one day the man who had been rich became poor. With a hand shaking with age and sorrow he wrote the following letter to Judah ben Bezalel studying in Poland:

„Dear son, you were engaged to my daughter Perl and I promised I would provide her with a dowry. But my business was afflicted with disaster. I lost everything I had. Therefore I can't keep my word. As you are now eighteen, and according to our custom you should marry at this age, I absolve you of your engagement, so you will not be prevented from marrying someone else.“

Judah answered from Poland that he was not in a hurry to marry and intended to keep his promise. But if his fiancée made a different decision and found another bridegroom, he would recall the engagement and not restrain her.

The time passed. The brave Perl set up a little bakery in the Jewish Town, to support her old, needy parents. Judah was immersed in his books. And the time was passing.

One day, military troops who were returning from war, passed through Prague - dusty, weary soldiers of cavalry and infantry.

One rider strayed into the streets of the Jewish Town. As he was looking for a way back, he rode into the lane where Perl had her bakery. The hungry soldier smelled the warm bread, stopped the horse and, without dismounting, reached with his lance and picked up one of the loaves lying on the board outside the shop. He wanted to turn the horse and gallop away immediately, in the manner of a soldier, without paying for his gain. But Perl noticed what was happening. She ran out of her shop, threw herself before the rider, and grasped the horse's bridle. Screaming and crying, she asked the rider to pay. With her paltry earnings she must support her mother and father, so let him at least take pity on them.

"I haven't had bread for three days," said the rider, "I don't want to die of hunger, after I escaped death on the battlefield. I have no money, but I can give you this roll of cloth as a pledge."

The rider unbound the coiled cloth from the saddle and handed it to Perl.

"If I don't come back by the evening to pay you, keep this cloth for your bread and enjoy its benefits," said the rider, spurred on the horse and disappeared in the crowded street.

Perl stored the cloth and waited a day, two, a week, a month. The rider did not come back. Finally she decided to use the cloth. She unwound it slightly and stared. A few golden ducats fell from the cloth. The more she unwound the roll, the more ducats sprang from each fold. When she had completely unrolled it, a heap of gold shone on the table.

Perl called her parents and all three rejoiced over the unexpected fortune.

Father Samuel sat down and wrote a letter to Judah living in Poland. He spoke about the miracle that had happened to his daughter Perl. The rider must have been the prophet Elijah, wrote Samuel, who else could have performed such charity to poor Jews? Now, my son, there is nothing to prevent you and Perl from turning your engagement into marriage.

Judah ben Bezalel returned to Prague and married Perl. His wife is said to have been a pearl among women.

Soon after his return Judah became a rabbi of Prague and everybody knew him by the name Löw. For his tall stature and great scholarship he was also called by Prague Jews High Rabbi Löw. But the scholars of his time called him a lion among the learned, a comfort to the eyes, and the breath of life.

In earlier times the plague death entered the towns on many occasions. It did not need a gate for entering. No town wall could stop it. In the morning a man got up strong and healthy, but in the evening he lay weak, with a sign of death in his eyes. The plague did not choose and took away both the young and the old. The grave-diggers were not able to dig enough graves in the cemetery. People were being buried even at night, by the light of torches.

In the country, entire villages were dying out, and in towns entire families, houses, lords and non-lords, masters and servants, all died. The noblemen vere running away from the towns afflicted by the plague to distant castles, but did not know if the plague death had got into the carriage with them.

Heaven punishes us — said some, and looked for the culprits. Others blasphemed and threatened Heaven. Still others accused the Jews of the contagion. They were said to have had poisoned the wells. But the plague took its toll of both Christians and Jews.

At the time when High Rabbi Löw lived and taught in Prague, the plague death afflicted the Jewish Town of Prague. It spared the other districts. Only children were dying in the Jewish Town at that time. The adults could only watch their sons and daughters leave them, while the cemetery filled with the dead. Great grief visited the Jewish homes. There was no family free from sorrow.

What have we done, cried the Jews, that we must bear such cruel punishment? They observed a strict fast to appease Heaven. But yet the children died. The angel of death circled over the Jewish Town of Prague and waved its mournful wings.

Late into the night Rabbi Löw perused his books and searched in his memory for a way to help. Faced with such immesurable dying, all his learning seemed to him a grain of sand in the unbounded sea. He felt sad because he knew that the youngest Jewish generation would die out if he did not find some remedy.

He went to bed late and slept restlessly. A soon as he fell asleep, the prophet Elijah appeared and motioned him silently to rise and follow him.

The rabbi got up and followed the prophet through the quiet streets of the Jewish Town, to the cemetery. In the moonlight he saw, as if behind a whitish cobweb, the fresh wet earth on the tombs of the children who had died that day. Then the clock on the tower of the Jewish Town Hall struck midnight. With the first strokes of the clock the earth was given life. It started to move, and lumps of clay began to rise. The earth opened and the children rose from the newly covered graves. They ran about the cemetery, jumping and dancing, as if rejoicing over the short freedom granted to them at the midnight hour. Rabbi Löw turned round to see the prophet Elijah, who stood by the entrance to the cemetery, tall and serene, but his outlines were misty, and he dissolved in the air. The rabbi opened his mouth to ask the prophet what it all meant, but he could not utter a sound. Anxiously, he woke up. He lay in his bed again. All around was the darkness of the night.

Rabbi Löw could not fall asleep again. He kept thinking about the dream until dawn. With the new day came a decision. Among his pupils, there was one he knew that was not easily frightened. He had him called.

"I know that you are brave," he greeted him, "that's why I have chosen you to help our Jewish community. We are being punished and we don't know why. There is only one way to know. Tonight you will go to the cemetery. Don't be afraid, the prophet Elijah will be standing by you, although you will not see him. At midnight the cemetery ground will start moving, the earth will open, and the children who have died in recent weeks will rise from their graves. They will run and dance among the tombstones in their white little shirts. Hide well and watch. When one of the children dances towards your hiding place, tear off its little shirt and hurry with it to me. I will be waiting for you."

The pupil promised that he would do everything as the rabbi had ordered. At night he went to the cemetery, hid behind a tombstone, and waited. As soon as the tower clock started to strike midnight, the ground of the tombs moved and the children got up as if after a long sleep, rubbed their eyes, stretched themselves, and started dancing. The pupil recognized familiar faces among them and his heart throbbed. The children's dance became more and more lively and wild, and soon they were dancing and jumping all over the cemetery. Some danced also by the tombstone where the pupil was hiding. Each time he would reach out his hand towards the dancing child and try to unlace the string of the shirt and take it off. But his fingers shook with excitement and each child would slip out of his grasp and dance away. Only when he tried his luck for the seventh time, did he manage to catch hold of the little shirt and take it off the child, without the child's noticing anything. Then he started for Rabbi Löw's house. The children kept on dancing, without having noticed him.

Rabbi Löw waited for the pupil at the door. He led him into the house and locked the door carefully behind him. Then they sat down in the living room, whose windows faced the street, and waited. It was dark inside, but outside the moon was shining on the empty street. The rabbi and his pupil waited for the clock to strike one. At one o'clock all the children would return to their graves. Only one of them would not be able to return, as it would not have its little shirt. All the children but one would find peace.

The clock struck one and the child appeared in the moonlit street. He ran to Rabbi Löw's house, knocked on the window with his tiny finger, moaned, and asked:

"Have pity on me, good people, give me back my little shirt. I can't come back without it and find peace."

"We'll give it back to you," answered the rabbi, "but first you must tell us why so many Jewish children are dying."

"Take pity on me and give me back my shirtie," cried the child.

But he did not want to tell why the plague raged in the town.

"All right," said the rabbi, "if you don't tell me why the children are dying, I won't give you your shirtie."

The child started crying and could not stop. The pupil almost took pity on him and gave him his shirt. But High Rabbi Löw knew that lives of other children depended on the child's answer, so he let him cry. All of a sudden the child stopped sobbing and said:

"Down in that street, in the house with the sign of a pitcher above the door, live two women who called the angel of death. They had secretly killed their children. Since that time the angel of death has not left the town."

As soon as the child had said what the rabbi wanted to know, he got back his shirt and ran away with it to the cemetery.

The next morning Rabbi Löw ordered the two women to be sent to him. They soon confessed their bad deeds. They were tortured by their conscience and desired a relief. They were called up before the court of justice and sentenced to death.

Once the punishment was carried out, the angel of death left the Jewish Town of Prague. And Rabbi Löw's reputation continued to grow.

At the time when High Rabbi Löw served in Prague, there was a wealthy merchant in the Jewish Town. He had several chests full of rare fabrics and dishes full of gold and silver. But he had only one son, Jacob. The old merchant gazed with fondness at his son from the darkness of his shop; he was running about in the sun, well-developed and as nimble as a mountain stag. As the boy grew, his mind developed very quickly. Soon he surpassed his fellows with his spirit, and differed from them like an apple-tree from unfruitful trees. Rabbi Löw noticed the lively merchant's son, and chose him for his pupil when he was only twelve.

The merchant did business with tradesmen from discant foreign countries. Men dressed in eastern style met in his shop. The fragrance of precious oils and wonderful spices spread around them, as though the breath of foreign flowers from distant gardens was carried in the folds of their burnouses, and followed them wherever they went.

Two of the foreign tradesmen came to visit the merchant every year. He became used to their visits and always expected them at their usual time. Jacob expected them too. They never forgot to bring him some gifts. And with the gifts he dreamed about the distant countries where flowers had a different fragrance, since they were closer to the rising sun.

Each day Jacob learned something new from Rabbi Löw. With the passing years he progressed with his learning like a pilgrim walking through a forest where the darkness recedes before the growing light.

Years passed, and the tradesmen continued to come and go. One year they arrived unusually early and came up to the merchant with an unusual request.

"Your son is growing up," they said, "and in our distant country there is a daughter of a rich man. We talked to him about your son. We told him how prudent and wise he was and what a good bridegroom he would be for his daughter. Before we left, he asked us to make a deal with you. He wishes that his daughter be engaged to your son. She is all he has. After he dies, all his riches will belong to Jacob. The girl is as graceful as the dawn above the waters. It is hard to decide which is more beautiful: her face or her soul. If you trust your friends and don't doubt that we really are your friends, you can remain calm and give your consent to the engagement. Your son is very fortunate."

"Allow me three days to think it over," answered the merchant in surprise.

The tradesmen agreed.

For three days the merchant could not sleep for worries.For three days he tried to find out who the rich man in that distant country could be.

He learned that there really was a rich man who had an only daughter, much gold and many precious stones. But this knowledge did not satisfy him. He visited the famous Rabbi Löw and explained to him what the foreigners wanted and what he had learned.

"If things are as you tell me," said the rabbi, "then you

have no right to keep your son from the path that offers him happiness. Don't worry about him. He is good and fair. The Lord has never abandoned such as him."

The merchant returned home, appeased,called his son, and disclosed to him what the foreign tradesmen had discussed with him and what Rabbi Löw had advised him to do.

Jacob was not against going with the men, who had always been kind and generous to him.

On the fourth day the tradesmen came back to have the answer. When they had the merchant's consent, the elder of them said:

"I am the rich man we talked about, and your son is to marry my only daughter."

The merchant was glad that he had made the acquaintance of the bride's father, and said to himself that it was better to give his son to somebody he knew than to somebody he did not. But whom among the people do we know well?

All the relatives were invited to the engagement feast. The feast was splendid. Everyone liked the bridegroom's speech and both tradesmen praised especially his ingenuity.

The following day Jacob was to leave his parents and his home, and to go with the tradesmen to the distant foreign country, where he would get to know his bride and let her know him.

It was difficult for his mother and father to part with their only son. Only the fact that happiness awaited him abroad helped them face his departure.

Early in the morning the tradesmen set out with him to the land where the sun rises. They wandered a long time.

Many times they saw the sun rise and set, but it did not rise and set above their destination. When they changed horses for camels, they said:

We are near our home.There is still a desert before us, one more day through the sands and rocks. When we pass through the desert, your will see, Jacob, beautifull landscape, which you have never seen before. In the middle of that landscape there is a white town. That town is our destination".

They passed through the desert and suddenly the landscape appeared before them, filled with emerald green meadows, groves and orchards. It its middle there was the white town.

Jacob cheered up, but his pleasure was not to last long.

As soon as the tradesmen arrived in the town, they took him into a big house with many floors and rooms. As they climbed the stairs, he could feel the presence of a sad shadow on each floor, in each room of that strange house. When they climbed to the top floor, they showed him a room where there were shelves full of scrolls and books waiting for him instead of the bride.

"What more would you like, my dear," said the elder of the tradesmen and spread out his arms in front of the bookcase, "sit down and search for the wisdom that is hidden in the books from other mortal men."

Jacob's heart throbbed when he sat down to the dusty books and scrolls. Far below him shone the white walls of the town and the gardens were green and full of sweet fragrances.

"Every day a servant will bring you something to eat," said the tradesman. Then he and his friend retired, shut the door carefully behind them, and locked it.

Jacob became a prisoner in the strange house.

His mother and father back in Prague thought about him and missed him. Days were growing into weeks, weeks were becoming months. The merchant of Prague began to worry about his son. He had been away from home for such a long time and there was no message from him yet.

Jacob passed the time with the books and scrolls and tried to understand, in vain, why the tradesmen who had always treated him kindly imprisoned him in the strange house and why they did not take him to his bride.

One morning he was sitting over his books again, when he heard a voice:

"Woe be to you, Jacob!"

He looked around but did not see anybody.

He sensed the presence of the same sad shadow as on the first day, when he had entered the house. The sky that he could see was shining like a blue flame.

"Woe be to you, Jacob," rang the voice again, "you will not leave this place alive, just as I did not."

Only then did Jacob notice where the voice came from. Beside the shelf with the books and scrolls there stood a marble column. On the column a human head could be seen, looking down on him. The head seemed alive. It moved its eyes and mouth.

"Woe be to you, Jacob," said the head for the third time, "you have fallen victim of evil people. Those two you came with, are not tradesmen but demons' servants. I was also a handsome young man, like you, and felt at home with books and scrolls. And you can see what happened to me. Every eighty years the servants of the demons find a learned young man, a first-born son of his father. They take his life and cut off his head. Then they put a label inscribed with Satan's name under the head's tongue. From then on the head has miraculous power. It can prophesy the future. The eighty years of my service will soon be over and you have been chosen to take over my position."

In terror, Jacob listened to the talking head. Only then did he realize that the pitcher of wine and the candles at the foot of the column were the sacrifices which the idolaters offered to their idol, the talking head. But he plucked up his courage and overcame his awe.

"You know what fate awaits me," he said, "and so you probably know too, which way I can escape from here."

"I know more than you can imagine," answered the head. "If you want to escape, you must do it tonight. But take me with you, or your captors will ask me about you and I will have to disclose to them where you are. Take me with you and do something for me. When you are among your own people, have me buried and pray for my soul."

As soon as the dusk fell on the town, the young man took the talking head in his arms and, on its advice, sprang out of the window into the depths of the darkness. He landed lightly on the grass below the town walls, as if he had wings.

At that moment Jacob's parents in Prague sat down to dinner and the light of the candle on the table expired.

"That is a bad omen," the father said, frightened, "our son is surely in danger."

He rose from the table and hurried to Rabbi Löw.

The learned rabbi ordered a fast and long prayers. Psalms and moaning rang through the synagogue. And then the musicians set shofars to their mouths, which are musical instruments made from ram's horns, and started blowing.

At that moment the window to the synagogue opened and Jacob landed at the feet of his teacher, Rabbi Löw, as if flown in by a favourable wind. He was invited to speak up.

He spoke about his journey through the desert, about the strange tall house, and about the foreigners who hid evil intentions behind their good-natured faces, just as a nut hides a mouldy kernel within its shell. Finally he showed the bewitched head to the congregation.

"Look," the rabbi called out, "Heaven has chosen this young man to overcome evil. He succeeded. Heaven does not abandon the righteous."

And High Rabbi Löw reached to the mouth of the talking head, took out the label with Satan's name from under its tongue, and tore it up.

"Go," he said, "and bury the head of this wretched man and accompany him to the realm of truth with a prayer for the dead."

Thus the talking head found eternal peace and the old merchant his beloved son.

## RABBI LÖW STOPS
## THE EMPEROR'S CARRIAGE

From time to time a smear campaign was raised against the Jews. The worst slander was that Jews secretly kill Christians and use their blood for their religious rituals

In High Rabbi Löw's time these slanders spread again and he saw in them a danger for the whole community. From bad rumours there was only one step to violence. How often unjust words gave strength to the arms to cause even more injustice.

At that time Emperor Rudolph II ruled over Bohemia. He resided in the Prague Castle, surrounded by courtiers and splendour, and also by scholars, astronomers, astrologers, and alchemists who sought the philosopher's stone, the magnificent primitive source of all life, animate and inanimate, the primitive matter which has even the power to change iron into gold, and to make people younger or even immortal.

Rabbi Löw decided to make his way to the court of Emperor Rudolph and ask the emperor for an audience. But it was not easy to gain such an audience, and the help the Jews needed against the slanderers could not be postponed. Therefore the learned rabbi chose a special way of asking for the audience.

On some days Emperor Rudolph II used to drive across the stone bridge, from the Lesser Town bank to the Old Town. Rabbi Löw knew about these days. As soon as such day came, he joined a group of curious people standing on the bridge, waiting for the show. Some of them had gathered there an hour earlier, so as not to miss it.

As the carriage approached, the news spread from mouth to mouth. The people greeted the emperor and thronged to see better. Rabbi Löw took advantage of the noise and turmoil. He slipped among the viewers and blocked the way for the carriage.

"Out of the way," called the people around the rabbi. He stood in the middle of the bridge like a stone set in the pavement. The carriage was quickly approaching until one could make out the silver trappings on the horses' harnesses. The hooves of two pairs of rare horses appeared near the rabbi, and he could see distinctly the face of the coachman, amazed and angry.

"Out of the way," the onlookers shouted at the rabbi again, picked up stones and pieces of hardened mud and threw them at him, in order to drive him away. But the stones and mud were transformed in the air and fresh and fragrant flowers fell at the rabbi's feet.

The emperor heard the unusual noise and looked out of the carriage window. Suddenly the horses stopped, as if a wall had grown in front of them. They were pulled up very close to Rabbi Löw.

He took off his cap and walked along the flower-strewn pavement to the carriage. He made a deep bow and asked the emperor for an audience.

The emperor, amazed at what he had just seen, graciously promised to receive him. Let him wait for seven days and on the seventh day let him stay at home.

On the seventh day the Jewish Town of Prague was excited by an unusual event. A marvellous court carriage arrived in front of High Rabbi Löw's house and the emperor's attendant raised the knocker on Rabbi Löw's door.

The rabbi was ready. The attendant opened the little door of the carriage for him, he stepped in, and to the astonishment of all who had rushed to the house, the carriage set out in the direction of the Prague Castle.

When the carriage arrived at the castle's courtyard, one attendant opened the little door and another took the rabbi to a spacious chamber where precious curtains ran down the walls, from the ceiling to the floor. Here he was welcomed by a nobleman from the emperor's company who offered him an armchair. The nobleman himself sat opposite him.

"The emperor is very busy," he said, "he asked me to attend to your matter."

The rabbi confided his worries to the nobleman. He defended the Jews against the slanders and explained the articles of the Jewish faith. He proved that any use of blood was forbidden to the Jews by their laws.

Suddenly the curtain parted and Emperor Rudolph stepped out of the recess where he had been hidden while listening to what the rabbi was saying, without being seen himself. He was pleased by the rabbi's wise speech.

"I will ask you one more question," he said to him, "if

you answer it well, I will take Jews under my protection. Answer me: are the Jews guilty of having crucified Christ or not?"

"Your Imperial Highness," said the rabbi, "let me answer your question with a parable. A powerful king had a son and that son had many enemies. They persuaded the king that the prince wanted to dethrone him. The king had him called up, but he, although innocent, did not utter a single word. Therefore he was brought to the court for trial. There were enough enemies among the witnesses, so there was no sense in his saying anything, and he kept silent. That was why the judges sentenced him to death. Only when the executioner's henchmen had brought him to the place of execution, did he turn to the place where the king would sit during executions, and asked him to avert suffering and death from him. But the king kept silent and the prince was executed. Who was more guilty: the judges or the king?"

"I understand what you mean," said the emperor, "and you can rely on my help."

The discussion between High Rabbi Löw, the emperor, and other invited noblemen lasted for three hours. Even the famous Danish astronomer, Tycho de Brahe, took part. He was to meet the high rabbi many times afterwards.

The court carriage brought Rabbi Löw back to his house in the Jewish Town. He was satisfied with his visit to the emperor's court. When asked if he had succeeded in the Prague Castle, he said:

"I brought back the emperor's promise that Jews must not be done any wrong. If any of the Christians has anything against a Jew, he will bring his suit before a legal court. The whole Jewish community must not be punished for the guilt of one Jew. From now on the rabbi and another representative of the Jewish community will go to the court with the accused Jew."

His words excited joy among the Jews. It seemed that an era of peace and justice was approaching. They looked up to the high rabbi with grateful respect and extolled him with the words of the Tanakh, the Holy Scriptures:

"Behold, the Lord loves a man of pure heart, and the king is a friend of a man of agreeable lips."

Emperor Rudolph still remembered his talk to Rabbi Löw. He remembered also the remarkable event on the bridge, when people had thrown stones at the rabbi and instead of the stones, flowers had been falling to his feet.

Who knows, he thought, maybe the learned rabbi can provide me another no less miraculous show. The emperor was anxious to have some special entertainment and to discover the secrets which, for common mortals, were locked behind nine locks.

Therefore he sent another carriage to fetch High Rabbi Löw. He stood impatiently by the window and watched for the carriage with the rabbi to appear in the courtyard. At last the carriage came and Rabbi Löw stepped before the emperor.

"I have heard that various magic arts are in your power," he addressed him. "I myself saw on the bridge that not one stone thrown at you harmed you. I have called you to fulfil my wish. I am having special guests in the castle and would like to show them something they have never seen before. Let us behold the primal fathers Abraham, Isaac, Jacob and Jacob's sons. Call them up by your magic power in front of my company."

"Your Imperial Highness," Rabbi Löw said, "it won't be easy to fulfil your wish. Give me time to prepare for such a difficult task."

"All right," consented the emperor, "the day after tomorrow I will be giving a feast and after the feast you will show us your art."

At the appointed hour, in the evening, a court carriage stopped again outside the rabbi's house, which pleased greatly all those who were sitting and talking in the streets.

The rabbi got in the carriage and started for the castle, whose lit-up windows shone into the darkness on that day. The courtyard was also more lively than usual. The servants were running about, the guards walking around. From the open windows one could hear music, talk, laughter and clinking of the glasses. The feast was ending.

The servants ushered him into a spacious hall in an uninhabited wing of the castle. Then they hurried to the banquet hall.

In a moment the spacious hall began to fill. The necklaces of the noblewomen and of the court ladies, and the rings of the noblemen glittered in the light of the candles. The exhilarated society was full of expectation. The emperor smiled at the high rabbi and motioned him to begin.

"Your Imperial Highness," he said, "before I start, I ask you to have all the lights removed. From now on, happen what may, no one is allowed to laugh."

The servants took away the lights and the hall got immersed in the darkness. But not for long. A white dim cloud appeared before the amazed society, quivering and sparkling like silver, changing its shape and dimensions, taking on a more and more human shape. Finally a gigantic old man, the patriarch Abraham, became visible. He paced slowly and graciously across the hall. His long beard was ruffled by the wind, although there was dead silence in the hall. Suddenly Abraham disappeared, as if he had entered the wall. And a new cloud appeared. The light figures of Isaac, Jacob and Jacob's sons, the Jewish forefathers, walked across the dark hall.

The emperor and the noble society held their breath.

They relaxed only when Jacob's son Naphtali appeared after the serene founding fathers of the Jewish kin. He was red-haired, freckled, and seemed to be jumping and running. The emperor burst out laughing and the noble society laughed after him.

As soon as the laughter was heard, the apparition disappeared in the darkness and the noble society heard muffled cracking and creaking of the wood above them, as if pieces of stone were grinding against each other. They looked up and in the light of the moon that had just left the dispersed clouds, they saw that the hall's ceiling started lowering. Turmoil broke out. Everyone wanted to save himself by fleeing the hall, but they were all in each other's way. Some looked in vain for the way out in the darkness, others just listened to the screeching of the lowering ceiling, stupefied with terror.

"Rabbi Löw, please, help us," called the emperor.

And the rabbi raised his arms against the falling ceiling and muttered some unintelligible words. The ceiling gradually slowed down. Then it finally stopped, as if striking some iron columns rather than the words.

At that moment the door opened. The servants entered with candles and showed the noble society out of the hall.

The lowered ceiling never returned to its original position. Since that time no one has visited the hall for fear that it might start moving again and bury curious people underneath.

## THE EMPEROR CALLS ON RABBI LÖW

High Rabbi Löw once dared to invite Emperor Rudolph II into his house in the Jewish Town. The emperor saw the Jewish houses in this part of Prague, when passing through those parts, so he knew how small they were. That was why he said:

"All right, I accept your invitation, but I will come with all my company."

He thought that he would embarass the rabbi. But he only thanked him for the honour he was doing him.

In no time the Jewish Town was in unprecedented agitation. The wheels of the emperor's carriage and the court carriages rattled through its narrow lanes. The horses' hooves were clattering and the riders' spurs were ringing. The emperor and his company stopped outside the house of Rabbi Löw. There was no place there because of the carriages, the horses' teams and the saddled horses. The large noble company doubted that the rabbi's small house would accommodate them.

High Rabbi Löw came out to meet them and ushered them to the hall of his house. They were paralysed with astonishment. They wondered how such a spacious hall with a stucco-decorated ceiling and wonderful tiles in the floor, which could match the tiles in any castle, could be placed in such a small house.

Rabbi Löw showed the noble guests from one hall to another and each was more beautiful than the other.

There were pictures, rare Venetian mirrors, marble tablets, carpets, gold and silver, all lustrous and glittering. The emperor was carried away by the splendour. He admired the precious vases and dishes, but above all he admired Rabbi Löw, who had conjured it up.

After having shown them the house, the rabbi invited the company to some refreshments. The ornamentally carved leaves of the big door opened by themselves and the guests could see a long table full of choice delicacies, crisp roast meat, sweet-smelling sauces, fancy sweets, refined wines. Although it was autumn, there were ripe, fresh fruits of the spring and summer, together with the autumn fruits, on the silver plates.

The guests ate and drank. Everything they saw and tasted delighted them.

In the emperor's company there was also a nobleman who could not find peace in the sight of such splendour. He did not enjoy it like the emperor and the other courtiers, but kept wondering what learning was necessary for one to acquire such singular, unheard of power. Therefore he decided to take something from the banquet table with him, in order to learn how all that splendour had appeared in the rabbi's house. When the emperor and his company were taking leave of the rabbi, the curious nobleman hid a golden cup under his coat and took it home with him.

Not only the Jews, but also the Christians talked for a long time about the emperor's visit to the Jewish Town. The rumour about the rabbi's extraordinary deeds travelled far beyond the borders of the town.

The nobleman watched the golden cup every day, but it remained always the same. After a few weeks, however, he heard a piece of news, remarkable and unbelievable. Somewhere in Moravia an imposing castle disappeared, together with all its furnishings, and returned to its place a few hour later, intact. Not a table-cloth, not a vase, nothing was missing. Only one golden cup had disappeared. As soon as the nobleman learned about this, it seemed to him that he found the key to the secret he was eager to understand. Immediately he went to see Rabbi Löw. He told him what he had discovered, and as proof that he was speaking the truth, he handed him the golden cup.

"I know," said the nobleman, "that you, Rabbi, are master of the secret Jewish learning, the kabbalah. You can't deny that. Teach me what you know. I am rich, have influential friends, and could be useful to you."

"Sir," answered the rabbi, "I can't teach you what you wish. Don't ask me why. Let's forget about your wish and let's talk about something else."

"Rabbi," cried the nobleman, "I am rich and have influential friends. I could use all that for you, but also against you. Beware!"

"I don't want to continue, sir, with the talk about the secret learning," said the rabbi, "but you force me to do so. Therefore I shall dare to ask you a few questions. Have you never done wrong to anyone in your life? Have you never done any injustice? Haven't you hurt any man, have you never caused anyone any pain? Are you really without guilt? Only he who is without guilt, only a good and just man, can know the secret Jewish learning. Only to him will it do good and not harm."

"I am absolutely without guilt," said the nobleman proudly.

"Look around you, sir," Rabbi Löw asked him quietly.

The nobleman looked around and turned pale. Behind him stood a transparent figure, as if woven from thin mist. In its face he recognized the features of his sister. Once, many years before, he had been the cause of her death, because he had wanted to get possession of her property.

Like a hunted man, the nobleman ran away from the rabbi's house. He never appeared in the Jewish Town again.

## RABBI LÖW JUDGES LIKE SOLOMON

Whenever it was necessary, Rabbi Löw's wisdom was of help to the Prague Jews, no matter if the injustice affected all of them, or if it concerned one single man. He knew well that wrong done to one man is like a spark. If we put it out in time, we often prevent a great fire.

At that time there used to be, in the Old Town of Prague, small shops under the stone arcades. Under one arch of such arcade there were two shops. A second-hand dealer and a pork-butcher sold their goods there, side by side. Their goods, as could be seen, were very different in nature, but their shops were partitioned only by a thin wall made of boards. The boards did not fit together, and the pork-butcher could watch easily the second-hand dealer through the cracks between the boards as he raked over old coats and caftans, and the second-hand dealer could also look through the cracks and see the pork-butcher weighing his sausages. The pork-butcher was a Christian and the second-hand dealer a Jew. But, as is often the case, the faith that one is officially registered with is not a certificate of the nature of one's heart.

One afternoon, when only flies visited the shops under the arcade, the pork-butcher put his eye against the cracks and watched the second-hand dealer. The second-hand dealer, who did not suspect that he was being watched, sat down calmly at his counter, shook his thalers from a pouch, smiled over them, counted them, put them back into the pouch, and locked it in the table.

From that moment on the pork-butcher could not find peace. He paced his shop and the thalers appeared before his eyes like sweet apparitions. His conscience held him back, but the Devil pushed him toward the door. And the Devil proved stronger.

He locked his shop and set out to a court of justice. He reported that he had been robbed, described the thalers, stated how many they were, and described even the pouch in which he kept them. He lamented over his immense misfortune and hinted that the little fortune must have been stolen by one of the shopkeepers in the arcades.

The guard searched all the shops and stores in the neighbourhood and eventually, at the Jew's shop, found a pouch exactly like the one the pork-butcher had described.

They arrested the Jewish second-hand dealer. He swore his innocence, cried, entreated them, but in vain.

Now the court had the pouch with the money and two owners, the second-hand dealer and the pork-butcher. They both claimed the pouch.

"You must have seen me counting my money," maintained the Jew, "can't you see everything that is going on next door through the cracks?"

"Oh, no," cried the pork-butcher, "the second-hand dealer saw me and my pouch, took it away from me, and he is making excuses now."

The judge did not know what to do. In such cases he asked the emperor to settle the matter. Emperor Rudolph liked to test the wisdom of High Rabbi Löw. He sent for him that time too, explained the matter to him, and waited with a smile to see how the rabbi would deal with the pork-butcher and the second-hand dealer.

Rabbi Löw reflected briefly and said:

"Your Imperial Highness, order a clean kettle to be filled with water and hung over a fireplace. As soon as the water in the kettle starts boiling, let a servant empty the pouch into the kettle."

The emperor was surprised at the rabbi's wish, but he ordered the water to be boiled in a clean kettle. As soon as the water started boiling, the servant emptied the contents of the pouch into the kettle. After a while the rabbi had the kettle removed from the fireplace and carefully examined the water's surface. Then he said to the emperor:

"Highness, the second-hand dealer is innocent. We all know that pork-butchers have greasy hands and that the money that goes through their fingers is stained with grease. But these thalers were in the hands of the second-hand dealer, who deals in dry rags. On the surface of the water there isn't a drop of the pork-butcher's grease."

The emperor liked the rabbi's proof and decided the case as Rabbi Löw had said. The rumour about the court of justice spread throughout Prague. The saying went that Rabbi Löw judged as wisely as the famous King Solomon.

The emperor's favour is said to have been inconsistent. He yielded to the advice and insistence of his counsellors and decided that in that same year all Jews should leave his country.

Representatives of the startled Prague Jews visited High Rabbi Löw to find assistance and consolation. He did not even let them speak, and said:

"Don't worry, the matter you are coming to me with will be solved within the night which is approaching."

The day drew to a close and it was growing dark. The first stars were lighting up dreams in sleepy children's heads.

The emperor fell asleep towards midnight and he had a dream.

He saw himself driving in a carriage, accompanied by his courtiers in carriages. The horses' hooves whirled the dust, the sun was burning hot, and the river alongside the road flowed in the shadow of the willows.

The emperor ordered his company to stop, got out of the carriage, hid in a bush and took off his clothes. Then he plunged eagerly into the river and began to swim. The sun above him burned in the blue sky and the water was pleasantly cool. The emperor forgot about his company. When he returned to the spot where he had entered the water, he saw his company stepping into the carriages, ready to leave.

His throat contracted with fright. He wanted to call to them not to leave, that he was not ready, but could not utter a sound. The carriages on the bank moved. A moment later, they disappeared in whirls of dust.

The emperor stepped onto the bank, looking for his clothes, but he could not find them. Sad and lonely, he sat in the grass and waited in the bush for the night to come, to be able to return to his palace in the darkness.

By night he set out on his journey back to Prague. He was not used to walking, his bare feet hurt him, and he was too far from the city. When he came to a forest not far from Prague, the day was just dawning. From the depths of the forest he heard the strokes of an axe. With the first hours of the day, the wood-cutters were the first to be at their work.

"Dear fellows," called the emperor from a thicket, "help me. Give me some clothes and something to eat. I'm your emperor . . ."

They did not let him finish the sentence and burst out laughing. He ran away from them. Ashamed, he ran to the end of the forest. He faced the imperial road to Prague. He hid behind a heap of stones and waited for somebody to notice him. Without his clothes, he did not dare to approach anybody.

By chance there was a beggar going along the road with a bundle of rags. The emperor, exhausted with fright and hunger, called to him. He asked him for a piece of clothing and something to eat. He forgot to boast that he was an emperor.

"Oh, my God," exclaimed the beggar, "I've only these few rags, but you're still poorer than I, you don't even have that." He took out a threadbare pair of trousers, full of holes, and a worn-out coat. He gave them to the emperor. He also shared a slice of bread with him.

On his way along the road, the emperor met familiar courtiers. He took up his courage and told one of them who he was.

"You, an emperor?" the courtier withdrew from him with loathing," poor wretch. The emperor is in his palace in the Prague Castle. I saw him with my own eyes this morning."

Now the emperor understood what had happened. Some cheat had seized his clothes, made use of his resemblance to the emperor, and left for Prague instead of him. Whom could he tell that he was the real emperor, when he was dressed in rags and his double in precious linen?

Meditating mournfully, the emperor arrived in Prague. He saw the burghers and their wives, the craftsmen and shopkeepers. They were all dressed better than he, the emperor. They are all happier than I am, the emperor thought bitterly.

He roamed about Prague aimlessly. His bare feet trod for the first time in the places where he used to travel only by carriage. All hope left him. With grazed feet he came to the Prague Ghetto, the Jewish Town. He thought of Rabbi Löw. He would certainly advise and help him. But how would he recognize his emperor in a ragged, barefooted beggar?

The emperor hesitated outside the rabbi's house and did not dare to knock at the door. Then Rabbi Löw himself appeared on the doorstep, bowed, and invited him to come in.

"Your Imperial Highness," he said when he had shown

him to his study, "I know what misfortune had happened to you and I shall help you. First I will have warm water and clean clothes brought. You must also be hungry."

The emperor washed, changed his clothes, and had his meal. When he looked at the kind face of Rabbi Löw, hope returned to him.

"Your Highness," said the rabbi, "King Solomon was once afflicted by the same misfortune as you. The king of demons, Asmodeus, took on Solomon's likeness and kept him from the throne for some time. Your place on the throne was also taken by a swindler who resembles you."

"But how shall I get rid of him?" the emperor interrupted the rabbi impatiently.

The rabbi smiled:

"The weather is hot and your double will go to the Vltava to have a swim. When he is in the water, do to him what he has done to you."

The rabbi described to the emperor the place where the false emperor would take a bath, and also told him the hour. In the end he said: "If you wish everything to come out well, you must do one more thing. He who wants to remove an injustice, must not do an injustice himself. Write out a document for your ministers recalling your decision that all Jewish people should move from your country."

The emperor wrote willingly the document, by which he revoked the banishment of the Jews. He confirmed his decision by a signature. Then he went to the Vltava's bank, where his double was supposed to come.

At the hour predicted by the rabbi the emperor's company stopped on the bank. The double got out of the carriage, hid behind a thicket and took off his clothes. As soon as he plunged into the river, the emperor put on what had belonged to him and hurried to the carriage.

The carriage moved forward and the emperor experienced a pleasure he had never felt before. At that moment he woke up. He looked around in confusion.

He was lying in his bedroom in the Prague Castle. All that he had experienced and suffered had only been a dream. He got up and walked about the room to make sure that what he was seeing at that moment was reality. But on the little table he saw the document he had written and signed, and on the upholstered chair there was a bundle of beggar's rags, to remind him of the poor and persecuted people, in whom he had found understanding and help.

The Jews remained in the country. The emperor altered his decision within one night, just as High Rabbi Löw had predicted.

It is said that four Jewish sages once entered the Garden of Eden, whose entrance is usually closed to common mortals. The first of them learned the Garden's secrets and died there. The second found the secrets of Paradise and went mad. The third lapsed from the faith of his fathers because he lacked the strength to understand. Only the fourth of the sages, the learned Akiba, went through the Garden of Eden without anything happening to him. Only he returned.

High Rabbi Löw was also said to have come through the Garden of Eden, just as the learned Akiba, and returned richer with the secret revelations. That was why the Jews trusted him, in difficult moments, as their saviour.

When the waves of hatred against the Jews rose again, Rabbi Löw was expected to help rescue them. They told him:

"Each night somebody can bring secretly a dead man to the ghetto and accuse us of murder. You can still find many people who believe the stories that we need Christian blood for our rituals."

High Rabbi Löw listened to the representatives of the community and nodded seriously:

"I am worried just like you," he said, "but don't be afraid, I promise to help you soon."

The elders of the Jewish community left, and Rabbi Löw

prayed long into the night, so as to be inspired with a dream and with good advice.

He went to bed late, and when he closed his eyes, a dream came to him. In the dream he saw an inscription running: Make a golem of clay — a figure similar to man. The golem will help you against your enemies.

The following morning, as soon as the rabbi woke up, he had his son-in-law and one of his pupils called immediately.

"I have called you," he told them, "because I received a command from Heaven in the night to make a creature of clay resembling man, a golem. We need four elements for this task: Earth, Water, Fire, and Air. I feel in myself the power of Air, you, my son-in-law, will represent the power of Fire, and you, my dear pupil, will represent Water. The fourth element, Earth, we shall find in a place favourable to our purpose. We shall part now. For seven days we shall be concentrating and preparing our minds in order to succeed in this matter."

For seven days Rabbi Löw, his son-in-law, and his pupil prepared for the unusual task. On the seventh day each of them bathed in the mikvah, the ritual Jewish bath, in accordance with the custom of their ancestors. Then they dressed in white clothes, and with a prayer on their lips, set out on their journey outside the city. The clock struck four, when the darkness is thickest, and brings to mind the moment before the creation of the world. Outside the city they found a spot on the bank of the Vltava, where there was enough intact wet earth, carried from the mountains by the river. They lit their torches and continued praying and reciting the Psalms.

They made a shape of a man, three ells tall, from mouldable clay. Then they put it on the ground, and by gentle movements of their fingers marked out its mouth, nose, eyes and ears, giving human features to its face. Then they imitated human legs, arms, hands and fingers. Finally the figure of the golem lay in front of them. It resembled a man lying on his back.

"You represent the element of Fire," said Rabbi Löw to his son-in-law, "walk round the golem seven times, while saying the lines I have written for you."

The rabbi's son-in-law walked round the golem, while saying the lines in a clear voice. When he made the first round, the golem became dry. When be made the third round, the golem glowed with heat. And when he was finishing the seventh round, the golem glowed and gleamed white-hot like iron in a smith's furnace.

Then the rabbi ordered his pupil who represented the element of Water to walk round the golem seven times too, saying his lines.

The pupil obeyed. During the first round the red gleam of the golem's trunk died out. When he made the third round, little clouds of vapour issued from the golem's surface and his body grew damp. During the following rounds, nails grew on his fingers, his head became covered with hair and his skin acquired a faint human lustre.

In his stature and appearance he resembled a man of thirty.

Then Rabbi Löw himself repeated the same procedure. During the seventh round, he opened the golem's mouth and inserted the shem, a parchment inscribed with God's name.

Finally the rabbi, his son-in-law and his pupil bowed to

all the cardinal points, while pronouncing together the following sentence:

"Lord made a man from the clay of the Earth and breathed the breath of life into his mouth."

After these words, life arose in the clay from which the golem had been made. Fire, Water and Air awoke him. He exhaled, and looked in amazement at those who had called him to life.

"Rise," Rabbi Löw ordered him.

And the golem rose, just as people rise after a long sleep. He straightened up and stood before his makers.

Now all that remained was to dress him. They had brought with them the clothes that were worn by the servants of the synagogue. They dressed him in these clothes, just as a person is dressed. They also showed him how to put on his shoes, and he did so. Now he looked like other people. He lacked only one thing - human speech. He was mute. Heaven kept the secret of giving the gift of speech to itself and did not share it with High Rabbi Löw. To perform the tasks for which the golem had been made, he did not have to talk. He was only to hear and obey.

The day was dawning and the red morning sky coloured the surface of the Vltava and the clay bed from which the golem had risen. It was time to return.

On the way back the rabbi said to him:

"We made you from clay and gave you life, in order to protect the Jews against their enemies and against persecution. I give you the name Joseph. You will live in my house and obey my orders. You'll do everything I order you even if I send you into the fire, even if I order you to throw yourself out of a tower, even if I send you to the depths of the sea."

Joseph nodded in agreement. He could hear and understand, but could not command his tongue.

That night three men had set out from the Jewish Town, but four returned. The rabbi's wife was just rising and wondered whom her husband had brought to the house. He was not allowed to tell her the truth.Therefore he said:

"I have met this poor mute man and took pity on him. I'll give him work as a servant of the synagogue and he can sleep in our house. But remember never to use him for housework. For it is written: Do not use the dish assigned to ritual purposes for everyday services."

The rabbi's wife consented and the golem received his corner in the house, where he would sit, cupping his chin in his hand, and wait for orders.

Before the spring festival of Passover, the rabbi's wife had much work. Rabbi Löw went out and the golem sat at home, calm and immobile, in the middle of the bustle. The rabbi's wife was passing his bench, cleaning up, preparing the festive meals, while the golem sat.

The tub in the hall was empty and it was necessary to bring in water. The golem is strong enough to bring the water and he just sits, she thought. Let him work. Just for once, it cannot do ony harm.

"Joseph," she addressed the golem, "go and fetch some water!"

The golem sprang to his feet immediately, took the pails and ran to the well. In the meantime the rabbi's wife went to the grocer's. The shopping took a little longer than she had expected. As she was coming back, she saw a great cluster of people outside the house. She came closer and stared.

Water was gushing out of their house's door. The street outside the house looked like a shallow river. There was water everywhere.

The people who gathered to see the unusual sight thought that Rabbi Löw had conjured up a miraculous spring in the house. They called the rabbi's wife to explain to them what it all meant. She thought immediately of the golem.At that moment he appeared, passed her by quickly, slipped through the crowd of the spectators, pails in his hands, and disappeared in the hall. In a moment he was outside again, wet from top to toe. He ran to the well with empty pails. Water gushed from the hall. Before the stream abated, the golem passed by the startled rabbi's wife again, with his pails full.

Rabbi Löw was returning home and saw at once what had happened. "You couldn't get a better carrier of water," she heard his voice behind her.

The golem was about to run for more water. The rabbi stopped him.

"Joseph! Stop bringing the water. We've got more than enough of it."

As the rabbi finished the sentence, the empty pails slipped out of the golem's hands, he turned towards the house and slowly, like a weary man, withdrew to his bench where he sat down and rested.

Then the rabbi said to his wife:

"Didn't I tell you that the golem could be used only for services pleasing to God?"

She kept silent. Instead of having less work, she had twice as much.

Experience is a rare spice, but in time it loses its fragrance and is forgotten.

An orphan girl had lived in the rabbi's family for many years. Rabbi Löw and his wife had taken care of her since she was a baby. When she reached marriageable age, they found a bridegroom for her. The rabbi saw to the dowry, while his wife took care of her trousseau. They prepared a wedding feast in the house, according to decorum. The house was in turmoil again. Everyone was assigned a task. Only the golem sat on his bench and rested.

The rabbi's wife worked in the kitchen and reflected: to

serve at the wedding of a poor girl is certainly an act pleasing to God. Why shouldn't I ask the golem for a service? It is still necessary to bring the fish ordered with the fisherman and to buy some apples. She remembered the flood which the golem brought about before the festival of Passover, but she soon stopped worrying about it. With fish and apples, he cannot do any harm.

"Joseph," she said to the golem, "go to see the fisherman who lives in the first little house by the Vltava. I have ordered some fish with him. Bring it here into the kitchen. Then you will go to the fruit market and fetch some apples. Take this note with you. Everything is written on it. It is enough if you show it to the fisherman and then to the people at the market.

The golem nodded in agreement and left the house.

The fisherman was mending his nets outside his little house. As soon as he saw the golem he realized why he was coming, even before he showed him the note. He brought the fish he had caught for the wedding feast, but didn't have a basket or a bag where to put it for the golem to carry.

When Joseph saw his hesitation, he seized the fish and put it under his jacket, which was girded by a belt. As he was of a tall stature, his clothes were large and the fish could be placed on his breast. Now only its tail was showing.

The journey back passed the river again and the fish felt the closeness of its home, from which it had been taken by force. It grew uneasy. All of a sudden it swang its tail fin and hit the golem on the chin. This provoked him. He took it from under his jacket and threw it into the Vltava, as a punishment. The fish disappeared beneath the surface immediately. The golem observed it with satisfaction and was glad that he was rid of it.

"Where is the fish?" the rabbi's wife asked him when he came into the kitchen.

By the gestured speech of the dumb Joseph told her what had happened. He had taken the fish, but it displeased him and he punished it. He threw it into the river and it was drowned.

The rabbi's wife only sighed and was sorry that she had asked the golem for help. In the bustle she forgot that she had set him one more task. But the golem did not forget.

He slipped out of the house and directed his steps towards the fruit market. He stopped near the stall with the apples and showed the note to the stall-holder. She weighed the apples, put them in a bag, and gave it to the golem. He looked at it scornfully. It seemed too small to him. He spread out his arms and suggested that he could carry far more. Possibly the entire stall, together with the apples and the stall-holder.

Passers-by stopped and smiled increduously. The stall-holder even burst out laughing. This outraged him. He raised her with his both hands above his head and set her on the apples. Then he put the entire stall, with the apples and the stall-holder, on his shoulders, and carried it straight away to the yard of the rabbi's house. In the yard he set the stall on the ground, took the stall-holder, half-dead from fear, off the apples and made her sit as she had sat in the market. She looked as if she were selling apples in Rabbi Löw's yard.

Only then did she recover and her voice returned to her. She burst out crying and cried so loudly that not only people from the house, but also people from the street rushed into the yard. The golem withdrew silently to his place in the house. He was convinced that he had done the work as well as he could and did not care what the others said.

It took a little while before the stall-holder stopped yelling. With tears in her eyes, she told everyone who was around her what terror she had felt when the golem carried her, together with the stall, on his shoulders, through the streets of the Old Town so that she soared between the sky and earth like a bird.

Then the rabbi then said to his wife:

"Didn't I warn you that we could use the golem only for services pleasing to God?"

She did not protest and kept silent. She was determined not to give the golem any other order and not to notice him, no matter how much work might be in the house and no matter how pleasing to God the order might seem to her.

It is said that even High Rabbi Löw himself once made a mistake.

Before the Jewish New Year called Rosh ha-Shanah, which was celebrated on the first of September by the Jewish people that year, a great wind raged.

The rain splashed on the streets of Prague and on the river with such force that those who did not have to leave their homes did not do so. Not a single fishing boat set out on the Vltava. Far and wide there was no fish to be had.

Then the rabbi thought of the golem. He would not be harmed by wind or water, and might catch some fish for the festive occasion. It certainly is not an everyday service.

"Joseph," he said to the golem, "here is a bag and a net, go and catch some fish."

The golem took the bag and net and set out into the wind and rain without delay.

In the afternoon some people from the country brought a carp to the rabbi. The rabbi's wife got to work in the kitchen, preparing the fish, and he forgot about the golem. Only late in the afternoon, at the hour when he would set him a task for the next day, did he think of him, wondering if he was still outside. He sent a servant to fetch him.

"Tell Joseph," he advised him, "to stop catching fish. He can return home even if he hasn't caught any."

The servant went to the Vltava. He did not have to search a long time.

The golem stood in the river and laid a net in the water. On the stone beside him there was a big bag, full almost to the brim with fish.

The servant cupped his palms around his mouth and shouted against the wind to the golem:

"Joseph, you must return. You can come home even without fish."

As soon as the golem heard that, he seized the bag with the fish and turned it upside-down, so that none remained in it. With the empty bag and net he waded through the river to the bank.

When High Rabbi Löw learned about it, he said to his wife Perl: "You see, I was trying to teach you and I have not taught even myself."

Each night Rabbi Löw sent the golem out to keep guard in the streets of the Jewish Town and the neighbouring Old Town of Prague. If he saw something suspicious, if he found someone who was about to harm the Jews, he was to intervene immediately.

Especially before the festival of Passover, when fabrications spread more than usual among the Christians, he paid close attention to everything that was going on in the Jewish Town and around the ghetto during the night.

He used to go on his rounds, disguised as a Christian porter. When an unusually difficult task was assigned to him, High Rabbi Löw would hang an amulet around his neck, with secret signs written on deerskin. The amulet made him invisible. Unseen, he would enter the taverns of the Old Town and listen to what the people were talking about. Unseen, he would punish those who deserved punishment.

At that time a Christian maid disappeared from the Jewish Town. During the Shabat when it is forbidden to Jews by the Jewish code to work in any way, the Christian maid used to help in the Jewish households. But now she was away and nobody knew where she had gone.

A few days after the maid disappeared, a daughter of a Jewish physician, named Dina, ran away form the ghetto.

The two disappearances were not connected at first.

But they involved a danger that threatened the whole Jewish Town.

The physician's daughter ran away to a near-by monastery. For a long time, she had been dealing in secret with the monks. She wanted to give up her Jewish faith and to accept that of the Christians. Her flight stirred Prague. The Christians and the Jews were excited even more by what she was saying.

A high religious dignitary gave her a long hearing as was routine in such cases. He asked her why she had decided to abandon her Jewish faith, and also asked her about her life. Dina answered willingly. She wanted to deserve praise and admiration in the new faith. Therefore she thought she had to taint with slander the people she had come from.

"Tell us," asked her the priest, "is it true that Jews use Christian blood for their Passover breads?"

"Yes, it's true," the girl consented eagerly.

"Perhaps you know," the priest inquired further, "where the Jews took Christian blood for baking their Passover breads this year?"

Dina thought for a while.

"How could I not know," she said. "Before the spring festival a Christian maid disappeared from the Jewish Town."

"Consider well, daughter, what you are asserting," said the priest.

Then, to add some weight to what she was saying, the Jewish girl Dina swore solemnly that she had heard with her own ears the conversation between the two servants of the synagogue, Abraham Chaim and Joseph.

"But Joseph is dumb," said the priest.

"He is," she said, not put off, "but he speaks with his hands better than with his tongue. They must have talked about that maid and how to take her life."

On the day when Dina had cast a terrible suspicion on the Jewish community, High Rabbi Löw learned about her statement and grew sad. A great trouble is set upon the people, he thought, and a great weight burdens the sons of Abraham. A verse from the Bible was called to his mind: "As a moth rises from clothing, so rises evil from a despicable woman."

But it was necessary to act without delay. He suspected that the guard would first come and arrest Chaim and Joseph. He decided to save Joseph at all costs. He needed him for a very important task. Therefore he hid him in the recess of his house and dressed another dumb servant in his clothes. He hoped that the judges before whom the dumb servant would be brought up did not know the golem's real face.

As soon as he managed to settle what was important, the bailiffs came. Abraham Chaim was already with them. Now they were coming to arrest Joseph. But they took away the false one.

Rabbi Löw felt relieved. He had succeeded in solving the one problem, but another remained.

He freed the golem from the recess, dressed him in rustic clothes, and gave him a letter.

"Joseph," he said, "you'll search Prague. If you find the Christian maid who served in the Jewish Town, you'll give her the letter and bring her back with you. If you don't find her in Prague, you'll search the surroundings of Prague, if you don't find her there, you'll search all of Bohemia."

And the high rabbi explained to the golem what disaster would befall the Jewish Town if the maid did not come back in time.

He nodded that he understood. In everything that concerned the protection of the Jewish community, he was keen and lively. He had been made for this purpose, just as the song- birds were made for singing, the bright day for work, and the dark night for sleep.

The rabbi handed him the letter. In the letter he asked the maid, in the name of her mistress, to come back quickly. If she had lacked anything before, he would make it up to her. In the meantime, he was sending her twenty-five thalers as a compensation.

The golem left the rabbi's house. There followed a long period of waiting.

Meanwhile, the day of the trial was approaching. Rabbi Löw was summoned to represent the Jewish community in the court of justice.

Although he was wise and eloquent, he was afraid that this time he would not be able to do much if the golem did not find the maid to disprove the slanders with her presence.

All Prague synagogues were busy on those days. The Jews were praying to avert the impending danger. If they lost, they could expect vengeful crowds, looting and murdering, to invade the Jewish Town, just as at the time of the scholar and poet Avigdor Karo.

The day of the trial came and nothing was heard of the golem. Rabbi Löw ordered a strict fast, but Heaven would not have mercy.

The dawn of the fateful day caught him by the window. He was still hoping that the golem would appear somewhere in the street and save them all. With the growing light the rabbi's hope diminished.

On that day there was a glorious service in the Altneuschul, or the Old-New Synagogue. It reminded people of the Day of Atonement. They forgave each other their sins, and worry and sorrow joined with weeping under the vault of the synagogue. Yet the Jews left the synagogue fortified by the words of Rabbi Löw.

A working day started. The sorrowful duty to take part in the trial fell on High Rabbi Löw and on the mayor of the Jewish Town, Mordechai Maisel. Victory in the controversy was out of the question. There was no trace of the golem, nor of the maid.

A great mass of people gathered outside the building where the trial was to take place. As soon as the physician's daughter Dina appeared with her escort, one could hear rejoicing and cries of enthusiasm. After her the mayor Maisel and High Rabbi Löw passed through the crowd. The people started to murmur, threats were falling from all sides, as a prelude to the evil which loomed before both Jews.

As soon as they entered the court room, the eyes of all people turned to them and watched them, as though they were guilty of all secret and horrible acts.

The judge began the trial and ordered to bring up both servants of the synagogue: Abraham Chaim, who really was who they thought, and a dumb servant, allegedly Joseph. Both were accused of the murder of the Christian maid who had disappeared from the ghetto.

Then the judge ordered the most important witness to be called up, the physician's daughter Dina. He asked her:

"Do you recognize the Jewish servants? Are they those you had heard talking about killing the Christian maid?"

"How could I not recognize them," Dina said. "One is named Abraham and the other Joseph. It was them who boasted of having killed the maid."

After that statement the judge reflected for a while. And then, into his thoughts, in the silence of the room, a quickly moving peasant's carriage rattled through the open window. The rattle came to a sudden stop outside the entrance to the court building. Soon both wings of the door flew open and the golem appeared in the room, holding firmly the hand of the missing Christian maid. Puzzled by the mass of people in the room, he searched excitedly after the seat where High Rabbi Löw sat. But he had already risen. He motioned to him. The golem started towards him and, using gesture language, told him everything he had gone through.

He had not found the maid in Prague, nor in the villages that were indicated to him by her acquaintances. He had to go and see her brother at the other end of Bohemia where she had gone visiting. As soon as he met her, he gave her the letter and made her brother take her to Prague as quickly as possible. If they had not had to take a rest because of the horses, they would have arrived earlier. They went to Rabbi Löw's house, and the rabbi's wife told them that they would find her husband here, in the court. So now they are here, and Heaven be blessed for that.

The court room murmured with amazement. The people pointed at the missing maid and at Joseph. The court had to accept such proof. Dina turned pale and looked in dismay first at the real and then at the false Joseph.

Then High Rabbi Löw began to speak. He pronounced one of his best speeches before the court. He stressed that Dina's case was an example proving how a lie digs a grave for itself. He fought passionately against slanders and stated that it was a narrow escape; a great injustice could have been easily committed.

The accused servants of the synagogue, the real and the false, returned, together with Rabbi Löw, the mayor Maisel, the happy golem and the Christian maid, to the Jewish Town.

With their return quiet and peace were restored to the Jewish homes.

## RABBI LÖW CALLS UP A SPIRIT FROM THE GRAVE

At that time two rich friends lived with their families in a big stone house in the Jewish Town of Prague. They both traded in the same kind of goods, and helped each other in business. Because they were able, honest and sincere, their wealth grew from year to year.

Their riches grew with their families. But the family of each grew in a different manner. One businessman, nicknamed Red-Head because of the colour of his hair, had strong and healthy children. The other, who was nicknamed Black for the same reason, had weak and sickly children. One had mostly boys, the other only girls.

The businessmen were still good friends. But the wife of the black-haired man often felt envy when she saw her neighbour's strong and healthy children. She did not show it, though. For the most part she regretted that she had not given birth to a boy. It was her warmest wish to have a son.

Then it so happened that both the wife of Red-Head and the wife of Black expected the birth of more children. Both households were preparing for that glorious moment. Red-Head's wife expected the child with joy and without fear. Black's wife looked to the future with anxiety.

Only old Esther who would come to Jewish houses to assist women in travail knew about her desire and worries. She often visited the stone house of both businessmen. Sometimes she would be with Red-Head's family, and other times with the family of Black.

One night both women gave birth to boys. Old Esther wished that Black's wife had had a strong boy, but the infant was very weak. To Red-Head's wife a strong and healthy boy was born. Old Esther helped both women and felt sorry that the handsome and strong son had been born to a family where there were already a few strong boys, and the weak and fragile son to a family where there were only girls. And so it occurred to old Esther to alter the intentions of Heaven.

When the women in childbed slept, Esther could be seen leaving a bedroom, carrying a living burden. Hidden in the darkness of the night, which had covered many an unfortunate deed in the past, she switched the boys in the cradles.

The time was passing. One year changed into another. The night when Esther replaced the children was past. Both boys grew up like palms and old Esther bowed to the earth. One day she lay down, and death took her away together with her secret.

Years were passing, and the time for the young men to get married arrived. The businessmen made an agreement that the only son of Black would marry the daughter of Red-Head. They started preparing a glorious wedding, as fit and proper for a son and daughter from such families. High Rabbi Löw was to marry the betrothed couple.

On the appointed day the bridegroom and bride stepped before Rabbi Löw in the yard outside the Altneu Synagogue, where the wedding canopy had been set up. When, under the canopy, the rabbi raised a silver cup with wine in order to pronounce a blessing, the cup slipped out of his hand and the wine spilled all over the floor.

The rabbi got frightened, but he overcame his emotion and motioned the servant Abraham Chaim to fill the cup again. Abraham took the bottle, but it was empty. Therefore he whispered to the golem to quickly bring another bottle from the rabbi's cellar.

He started to run toward the cellar, but stopped outside the synagogue, as if held by an invisible force. Then he changed a direction and ran into the rabbi's house.

Abraham and the guests did not understand what the golem's strange behaviour meant. In the meantime he ran into the rabbi's study, took out a piece of paper and a quill, and wrote:

"The bridegroom and the bride are brother and sister."

He ran back to Rabbi Löw with the piece of paper. He read the note, looked at the agitated golem and asked him:

"Who told you?"

The golem motioned the rabbi to follow him. He stopped in front of one window of the synagogue and pointed upwards. A spirit stood there, which had told him who the bridegroom and the bride were. The rabbi saw the spirit, but the wedding guests did not. The spirit looked mournfully at the wedding gathering for a few more moments and then dissolved in the air.

Rabbi Löw came back to the wedding-guests and said:

"It's necessary to postpone the wedding. We must settle an important matter, which will be to the benefit of the bridegroom and the bride. Since the wedding is being postponed, give the wedding meals to the poor. Don't be sad. It is better to bear a short suffering and be merry all

70

your life than to experience a short joy and suffer for the rest of your life."

The wedding guests parted and Rabbi Löw sat down to his books in his study.

The following morning he sent the golem for a carpenter and ordered him to set up a wall of boards in the corner of the Altneu Synagogue. When the Jewish community gathered in the synagogue for the service, the rabbi asked them to stay in their places after the service.

After the end of the service he went with the families of both businessmen, including the bridegroom and the bride, to the wooden wall. Auxiliary judges sat down beside the high rabbi. He called the golem.

"Joseph," he told him in front of the whole gathering, "take this stick and go to the cemetery, to the grave of the deceased Esther. Strike the ground that covers her with the stick and wake her soul. Then let her come among us."

The Jews gathered in the synagogue were seized with terror.

The golem came back soon. A great silence went in front of him and behind him, as if the silence of the dead accompanied him. He passed the stick to the rabbi and pointed to the wall of boards. The people gathered there held their breath. The soul of the deceased Esther, having been called up from the grave, stopped behind the wall.

The rabbi's voice rang through the dead silence:

"We, the earthly court of justice, order you, Esther, to tell us how it happened that this bridegroom and this bride were marked out as brother and sister."

The spirit behind the wall began to speak. The rabbi, the judges and the families of both businessmen under-

71

stood every word, but the gathered Jewish community heard only indistinct, lugubrious and sorrowful mumbling. The ghost described the night when both boys were born, how she had switched them, and how, since the time she had died, twelve years ago, she could not find peace. Only because High Rabbi Löw was to marry the betrothed couple, was it allowed to her to prevent the marriage. If the brother had married the sister, her soul would have never found peace.

"Take mercy on my soul," moaned Esther, "mend what I have done wrong. If you don't believe the dead, go and look over my old notes. You will find them in a chest under the window of my daughter's home."

High Rabbi Löw sent the golem to fetch the notes. The substitution of the boys was written down in old Esther's papers. The rabbi consulted the judges and brought in a verdict:

"Because you, Esther, have done wrong to these betrothed, while alive, ask forgiveness of them."

Esther broke out sobbing and moaning behind the wall. She was asking forgiveness of the betrothed and none of the people in the synagogue could restrain their emotions.

She stopped crying and the high rabbi continued:

"We, the earthly court of justice, absolve you, Esther, and ask the heavenly court to grant you the grace of posthumous quiet and peace. Retire in peace and rest in peace until the day of resurrection."

After a while the high rabbi had the wooden wall removed, to prove that the soul of the dead woman had left the synagogue. Then, in front of the gathered Jewish community, he pronounced the engagement cancelled. But he suggested that the real son of Black should marry the girl he had until that time considered his sister, but who had proved not to be.

Both families welcomed his advice. Soon they arranged a wedding. This time nothing interferred with the wedding ceremony, and the young couple were able to find joy and happiness in their life together.

High Rabbi Löw called the golem after the wedding and ordered him to fasten one of the boards from the wall, behind which the soul of the dead woman had stood in the synagogue, to her tombstone. It remained there as a memory of the remarkable event.

Once upon a time, there was a ruin of an old castle not far from Prague. Those who had to walk or go by a carriage to Prague at night preferred a road as far from the ruin as possible. The ruin of the castle was said to be haunted by evil spirits.

Some people had heard a whole band playing in the full moon, as if the spirits were having a ball. Others had seen trumpeters blowing their trumpets on the crest of the roof, giving a signal to an attack. The travellers feared most of all a pack of black dogs which often rushed out from the castle's vault and ran, their muzzles on the track, as if following someone's trail. Everything in their way was swept aside. Furious barking resounded far and wide into the night.

One night a Jewish shopkeeper returned home that way. He had been doing business in the villages around Prague the whole day, and now he was looking forward to returning to Prague, to his wife and children.He did not want to waste time, and therefore chose a straight way below the ruin. He hoped that he would run along the path below the castle as quickly as possible. He saw himself at home already, rather than in the forest. Before he had walked half of the way, a big black dog sprang up from a heap of fallen rocks, fixed its sulfur-yellow eyes on him, and ran around him three times with terrible barking. Then it disappeared, just as it had appeared.

The poor shopkeeper gasped for breath from the shock. He staggered home half-dead, and his voice faltered as he tried to tell what had happened to him. His wife tried to comfort him, but he continued to be haunted by the yellow eyes of the dog, and the barking sounded in his ears until his head ached. He lay down and fell into an uneasy sleep.

Around midnight the shopkeeper's family woke up in terror. He lay in his bed and it seemed that he was asleep, but his mouth gave out terrible, persistent barking.

"Darling," his wife said and shook him up, "darling, wake up!"

The children started crying and shouting. Only then did he wake up. He looked around him anxiously, as if looking for somebody.

"What is it? What happened?" his wife asked him.

"Nothing, nothing," he comforted her. "It was only a dream. In the dream I was in a long line of soldiers. We all sat on black dogs. We drove the dogs to an attack and we all had to bark."

The shopkeeper was in a sweat from top to toe, and was almost too weak to move.

The following night he had the same dream. Again he was in an attack in a line of soldiers. They sat on black dogs and forced him to bark.

Since the meeting with the black dog he would wake the whole family by barking night after night. He grew visibly weaker and weaker. At night he was haunted by the image of the battlefield full of black dogs and during the day he could think of nothing but the previous night and the night to come. His legs could hardly carry him from his bed to the table, his business deteriorated. He could not imagine going from village to village on his business.

The shopkeeper's wife was worried, and could not even look at her husband for pity.He was dissolving before her eyes. She cried, and kept thinking how to help him. Finally it occurred to her to consult High Rabbi Löw.

He did not object to visiting the famous rabbi. He was so weak that he had to lean on his wife and his oldest son. Thus they set out, together with their other children, to ask Rabbi Löw for help.

"Tell me everything from the beginning and don't omit anything," Rabbi Löw said to him.

He told him what he knew, and his wife told the rest for him.

"Show me your tallit, which you are wearing under your clothing," asked the rabbi.

He showed him the garment which he wore under his clothing according to the custom of the Jewish men. It has fringes in accordance with the Lords' wish, since it is written that the Lord said to Moses: "Speak unto the children of Israel, and bid them make fringes in the corners of their garments throughout their generations, putting upon the fringe of each corner a thread of blue."

The rabbi examined the tallit katan carefully and saw that from one fringe two threads were torn off.

"How could you not be haunted," he said, "when you are stripped of protection against evil, and your angels have left you? First put your tallit in order."

Then he had an amulet of deerskin made and wrote on it the words from the second book of Moses: ". . . but not a dog shall snarl at any of the Israelites, at man or beast . . ."

"Every evening, before you go to sleep, you will fasten this amulet on your forehead," he said. "For seven nights you will sleep in the golem's bed and he will sleep in yours."

The shopkeeper did as the rabbi advised him. The golem's bed was a place of sound sleep. He always fell asleep whenever he lay down on it and never woke up before it was time to fulfil the first tasks of the day. The shopkeeper slept just as soundly as the golem. He did not wake, and each night gave him back some of his lost strength.

On the seventh night, High Rabbi Löw called up the golem and ordered him to take a bundle of straw, flint and steel, and set fire to the ill reputed ruin.

The golem fulfilled the order. Bright flames cleansed the fatal place and evil spirits fled from those parts.

After seven nights of undisturbed sleep, the shopkeeper recovered and could set out about his business again.

The golem was not able to remain idle for long. His day was scheduled for duties which he did as a servant of the synagogue, then his rounds, and evening keeping of the guard. Provided he had a while to himself, he would sit in his corner in the rabbi's house, cupping his chin in his hand, as if napping. As soon as the clock struck the hour when he was to do some task, he got up and went about his work.

Every day Rabbi Löw assigned him duties. But on Friday afternoon he assigned him in advance what he would do on the Shabbat. The Shabbat is the time of rest which the Jews kept strictly at that time. Rabbi Löw avoided giving orders on this holiday. The Friday order for the Shabbat was always the same. The golem was to keep guard and frustrate the intrigues of the enemies of the Jewish community. Although the Shabbat duty never changed, the rabbi had to repeat it each Friday.

Once it so happened that High Rabbi Löw left the house earlier than usual and forgot to give orders to the golem. He forgot about him even when he left for the synagogue to commence the Shabbat.

The golem was sitting idle in the rabbi's house for many hours and his strength was accumulating, like the water of a river constantly gathering behind a dam that stands in its way. Late in the afternoon he felt so much strength that it was impossible to hold him back. Like a madman, he broke out from the rabbi's house into the streets, sprang up and tore off shop-signs, broke and crushed everything that got into his hands — wood, stone, iron. Frightened people tried to escape him and locked themselves in their houses. Out of breath, they listened behind the doors, as he stamped up and down the street, tore up a tree with its roots, turned it with its top down and ploughed the street of the Jewish Town as a ploughman cuts furrows in the soil with his tracer.

Rabbi Löw had just started the Friday evening service in the synagogue with a song, when a messenger rushed in with the terrible news about the golem's rage. The rabbi thought for a while. The Shabbat had just begun, and from that time any kind of work is forbidden to the Jews for the entire holiday. But human lives were in danger and it is permitted to break the peace of the Shabbat in order to save them.

The rabbi went out of the synagogue and heard the din and the golem's panting in the streets of the Jewish Town. He could also hear the crying and moaning of the endangered people. He took a deep breath and, as loud as he could, called in the direction where the noise was coming from:

"Joseph, I command you, stop!"

At that moment Joseph stopped. The axe with which he had broken up the gate of the nearest house, slipped out of his hand. He stood like a big lifeless stone. Rabbi Löw came up to him and ordered:

"Joseph, go home, lie down and sleep. Tomorrow keep guard again and if you see anything suspicious, come and tell me."

The golem went home, silent and meek as a lamb. He

lay down and fell asleep, satisfied to have a new task ahead.

The high rabbi returned to the synagogue, had the festival song sung again, and thus started the desecrated Shabbat.

But he said to his son-in-law and to his pupil, with whom he had made the golem:

"Don't forget this event. Let it be a lesson to you. Even the most perfect golem, risen to life to protect us, can easily change into a destructive force. Therefore let us treat carefully that which is strong, just as we bow kindly and patiently to that which is weak. Everything has its time and place."

After many years the relations between the Jews and the Christians improved. The slanders about the Jews using Christian blood in their rituals ceased and the golem was no longer needed.

Then High Rabbi Löw said to him: "Joseph, tonight you will sleep in the attic of the Altneu Synagogue instead of on your bench in my house."

Then he sent Abraham Chaim, the servant of the synagogue, to fetch his son-in-law and his former pupil, with whom he had made the golem.

"You were present at the making of the golem," he told them when they had come, "it is necessary that you should be here at his end. We don't need his services any more. Therefore we shall meet tonight at two o'clock in my house. Together we shall dispel what we called to life."

In the evening the golem went obediently to the attic of the Altneu Synagogue and lay down to sleep. The window to the study of the rabbi's house was lit up late into the night. The Jewish Town Hall clock struck two o'clock of the new day. Only then the three men stole from the rabbi's house: High Rabbi Löw, his son-in-law and his pupil. The night was dark, just as at the time when they had made the golem. Life was to be extinguished in the darkness in which it had arisen. Darkness was to keep the secret of their act.

They climbed to the attic of the Altneu Synagogue. The

pupil was carrying a burning lamp. Its dim light touched the beams shyly. They looked around in the little circle of the yellow light and only in the other half of the attic did they discover a pile of old half-decayed synagogal textiles and Hebrew books, which had been brought there over the centuries by the servants of the synagogue. The golem had made a bed on the pile and now slept soundly.

"When we wanted to bring the golem to life," the rabbi said, "we were standing by his feet, facing his head. Now we shall return him back to the earth from which he had arisen. Therefore we shall stand behind his head, facing his feet. And together we shall recite backwards the sentence about the creation of man."

The high rabbi, together with his son-in-law and his pupil, stood up behind the golem's head and recited slowly backwards the sentence about the creation of man. His chest moved more and more slowly at their words, and it seemed that he was losing his breath. The rabbi bent over him and out took the shem from his mouth. At that moment his breathing ceased and he looked like a man whose life had gone.

Now the rabbi walked round the golem seven times in the opposite direction, reciting the lines. After him the pupil repeated the same procedure, and then his son-in-law, representing the element of Fire.

The pupil recalled the element of Water with his rounds and the golem's skin grew grey and brown as dry earth. The son-in-law recalled the element of Fire and the golem lost his solidity. He became brittle and began to disintegrate. He turned into what he had been before Rabbi Löw called him up to protect the Jewish community.

Thus he, for whom it was easy to reach for anything

that was ten ells above the earth and whom nobody could prevent from fulfilling an order he had received from High Rabbi Löw, turned to earth.

The clay figure, still resembling the golem, was stripped of its clothes, and covered with textiles and remnants of old robes and tattered Hebrew books. The rabbi passed over the clothes that were taken from the golem to the servant Abraham. The next day they were burnt secretly.

In the Jewish Town he spread a rumour that Joseph had disappeared from the town at night without a single trace. In all synagogues he announced that from that time on nobody was allowed to enter the attic of the Altneu Synagogue. He was afraid that someone might try to revive the golem to the detriment of himself and of all who lived in the Jewish Town.

High Rabbi Löw lived many years and during his life learned many things. He conveyed much of his knowledge and experience to his pupils and to the books he wrote. But also in the trail of the wise rabbi Death walked slowly and waited for her opportunity.

The years were passing and it seemed that Death could not catch up with the rabbi.

But she did not rest. The famous city of Prague was beset by the plague and the streets changed their appearance. People were driven into their homes for fear of the epidemic, or went to taverns, where they sought oblivion in immoderate drinking and wild dancing. There was no remedy against the plague. Those who trembled with fear at home, separated from the others, died, just like those who drank sociably and whirled in a dance. Both the old and the young died. But worst of all did the plague rage in the Jewish Town. The gate to the Jewish Cemetery was open day and night.

Sorrow over the plague disaster kept the high rabbi awake at night. He went out of his house during the night, wandering about the streets of the Jewish Town. The windows of the rooms of the dying were lit up. He would see the carriages of the dead coming back from the cemetery to fetch load after load, and hear the weeping of the widows and the crying of the parents. Neither the gates nor the walls could hold back so much lamentation. The wings of the unmerciful angel of destruction spread over the town.

On one of his nocturnal journeys Rabbi Löw came near the cemetery, where there was a commotion. New graves were being dug the light of torches. In the sad gleam he saw a figure standing at the gate to the cemetery, covered from head to foot. He stepped back to see who it was. In the gloom he recognized the sparkling feverish eyes sunken in the sockets, and the gaunt face where the bone was covered only by skin. He looked into the eyes of Death. She was holding a piece of paper in her bony fingers. On the paper were written the names of those who were to leave their families the next day, never to return.

The rabbi jerked the paper from the Death's fingers, crumbled it, and hid it under his cloak.

Death howled like a sorrowful autumn wind in the chimney and said:

"You might think that you have won, and yet I shall not forget about you."

High Rabbi Löw went home and read the names of those who were to die. There were many of them, for the next day was to be the Death's great day. Among the names he also found his own. When he had read all the names, he thoughtfully reached out his hand with the paper, close to a burning candle, and burnt it up. Then he rubbed the ashes between his fingers.

That night the plague ceased and destruction withdrew from the town. Everyone felt relieved. Life was returning to its old order.

Rabbi Löw knew that Death would not forgive him for what he had done. He watched his every step more carefully. Death took on various appearances, set snares for the learned rabbi and lay in wait for him in many different places. But he recognized her from a distance, and avoided her. He chose other ways in time, in order to escape her.

The years passed and the rabbi kept on winning over Death. And because he also shunned fame and dignity, both fame and dignity never left him. His relatives, friends and pupils gathered on his birthdays. There were many of them. He would sit in their circle and enjoy the quiet and peace which are brought by old age.

Once he was sitting among his relatives, accepting the congratulations of the guests. He was ninety-seven years old and his hair and beard were white as snow in the middle of the winter, but his eyes were still full of the kindly autumn light.

Suddenly the youngest granddaughter came up to the old rabbi and handed him a fresh rose. He took the rose and breathed in its fragrance for a long time. As he did so, his head sank and his chin leaned on his breast. He exhaled. The rose dropped out of his hand. Death was hiding in it and with her sweet smell she found her way into his heart. With cunning she overcame Judah, son of Bezalel, called High Rabbi Löw.

Rabbi Löw left the world of the living. His house, with a grape and a lion carved in the stone tablet above its entrance, became silent. Another shelter awaited him. His tombstone in the Old Jewish Cemetery resembles a little house with gables and a roof. Here rests Rabbi Löw with his faithful wife Perl.

From time to time a piece of paper with a prayer or a wish written by some visitor is slipped into the cracks of the tombstone. The place of his last repose continues to be visited by people's desires or anxieties. People appeal to his grace as they did in his lifetime. And so it remains until today.

One day, many years ago, a student who had dropped out of his studies came to Prague. During his studies he learned many things - something in Paris, something in Heidelberg, something of everything, but altogether nothing. He was attracted to Prague by something other than the famous Prague University. He had heard that the Jewish rabbis knew the magic of the creation of an artificial man. He read somewhere about a rabbi who had made a figure of a woman and inspired it with life. She served him in his household. He was accused of witchcraft, and was called up before a court of justice, together with the woman he had made. As proof that the figure was not a human being with a soul, he dismantled her into levers and wheels in front of the jury, just as a machine is taken apart. And when the student learned that Rabbi Löw of Prague had put his golem up in the attic of the Altneu Synagogue, he could not resist. If I had a golem, he thought, he would surely help me to money and a fortune, he would work for me and bring me everything I sent him for.

Greed and desire for such an artificial servant brought the run-away student back to his books. He gave up his beer-mug, searched in Greek and Latin books, and started even to learn Hebrew.

After some time, it seemed to him that he had found the right thing. Just like the learned Rabbi Löw a long time before, he made a shem which was to bring the golem back to life.

With the shem, and a few last kreutzers tinkling in his pocket, he arrived in Prague one evening and set out immediately for the old Jewish Town. He walked round and round the Altneu Synagogue and was sorry that the sun was not setting more quickly. He needed a dark night for his deed. Therefore he went to the nearest pub, ordered dinner with the last of his money, and looked forward to seeing the smiling face of luck soon.

From time to time he cast impatient looks at the window, waiting for the night to come. And when the night came, it remained only to count the hours.

At midnight the student went out of the pub and hurried to the Altneu Synagogue, hidden in the darkness, since that night neither the moon nor the stars shone. He could hardly recognize the synagogue. Unlocking the locks without a key was easy for him. He had learned the art of thieves and jesters better than any other.

In the attic of the Altneuschul he lit a candle and looked for the golem. Where else could he be than under that great pile of textiles, hundreds of years old, and tattered books? He put the candle on a brick and looked over the tattered textiles and papers hurriedly. All of a sudden, his finger slid in to some clay. He took off a few yellowish textiles carefully, and, suddenly, he could make out a body of clay, rubbed in some places, full of cracks. So! It was the golem of Rabbi Löw and neither the head nor the arms or legs were missing.

The student did not want to postpone his happiness. He put the shem quickly into the golem's mouth and waited for something to happen.

With amazement he watched the golem's cracks close up, the wounds made by the years, when nobody had entered the attic, heal, and the surface of his body toughen. His chest rose and descended slowly, then rose again. He was breathing. But he did not open his eyes. His head seemed to sleep, but his body was waking. He sat up and trembled. The student did not notice that. He was happy that the golem was moving, and that during that same night he would send him somewhere to get the money. He saw himself already a rich man.

And the golem got up, like a man who had been sleeping for a long time, but he did not open his eyes and trembled all over his body. With each vibration he grew up towards the rafters of the attic. He grew slowly, little by little. His body was rising like dough, even at the sides, and did not stop growing.

The frightened student tried to hold back the golem's growth. He raised his hands against him. But the clay dough kept on rising and ran through his fingers. The golem filled a quarter of the attic, then an entire half, and did not stop growing. He was losing the shape of a human creature and resembled a mountain of bubbling clay, without shape. One could still make out his head and his closed eyes. And then the student, frightened out of his senses, decided that he would rather give up the golem. He sprang to his feet and tore the shem out of his mouth. At that moment the golem stopped growing, life ran out of him, new cracks appeared in the immense mass of his body, as in dried-up clay. He bent to the ground and fell down.

Under the clay body the student encountered his death.

He was a run-away student, he knew something of

everything, though, altogether nothing. He had written an imperfect shem, which awoke the golem to imperfect life.

The golem of High Rabbi Löw was assigned to protect the humiliated people against wrong-doing. That was why good forces were present at his creation and helped him. The run-away student thought only about himself, and therefore the good forces left him. He was alone in the attic, and alone he remained.

# CONTENTS:

# Jewish Town of Prague

Prague used to be one of the most important Jewish centres in Central Europe and also an administrative, cultural and religious centre of the Jewish communities in Bohemia. Therefore the history of the Jewish community in Prague forms an inseparable part of the Jewish history of the Czech lands.

The oldest Jewish settlements on the territory of Bohemia arose in the early Middle Ages as merchants' stations at the junctions of trade routes. Their existence in Prague is recorded already for the middle of the 10th century, when the Jews settled near the prince's market in the settlement round the Prague Castle. In the second half of the 11th century, under King Vratislav, there appears a Jewish settlement round the Vyšehrad Castle, on the territory of today's New Town. This settlement was abolished soon, probably during the anti-Jewish riots connected with the first Crusaders' campaign in 1096—1098. For the first half of the 12th century there is proof of the existence of a Jewish community in the Lesser Town settlement round the Castle, whose synagogue burnt to ashes in 1142 and was probably never restored. Besides these oldest Jewish settlements round both Prague castles there also arose a Jewish settlement near the prince's market on the right bank of the Vltava in the middle of the 12th century at the latest, on the territory of the later Jewish Town. The small independent district around the Old Schul ⑦ is traditionally considered the oldest settlement in this area. Throughout its existence it remained separated from the ghetto.

In the 13th century, in the reign of Wenceslas I and Přemysl Otakar II, the Old Town was fortified and an extensive building activity developed on its territory. The Jewish settlement had to be arranged in a different manner because of the influx of new colonists, and its inhabitants began to be concentrated in the area around the Altneuschul ① which became a genuine centre of the Prague ghetto and kept this position in future. In 1254 Přemysl Otakar II issued a privilege for the Jews of Prague, where he defined, for the first time, their position as direct subjects of the king and promised them legal protection. They were allowed

# Jewish Town of Prague

to work only in trade and finance, and had to pay high taxes and grant special loans to the king. The Jewish settlement was converted into a closed ghetto at that time, separated from the surrounding city by walls and gates. Despite the protection promised by the king, many anti-Jewish riots and pogroms occurred during the following centuries, as a consequence of religious intolerance. Three thousand inhabitants of the ghetto were victims of the greatest pogrom that took place at Passover 1389. That is probably why there is no significant monument from the High Middle Ages in the Prague ghetto. Only at the beginning of the 15th century the Old Jewish Cemetery ③ was founded on the north-west periphery of the ghetto. It was used as the main burial place of the Prague Jewish community until the end of the 18th century.

After the death of Ferdinand I in 1564 there began, despite the efforts to banish the Jews from Prague, a period of the greatest economic and cultural prosperity of the Jewish community, which culminated in the reign of Emperor Rudolph II. In 1577 he confirmed all the privileges granted to the community by the preceding sovereigns and promised the Jews that they would not be expelled from Prague in future. In 1585 he acknowledged that they were subjected to the emperor's judge and in 1599 he exempted the Jewish community from all customs-duties and tolls paid in the towns of Prague. The community gained its former autonomy at that time. The development of crafts and trade brought about a great revival of the ghetto and the number of its inhabitants multiplied. Mordecai Maisel (1528— 1601) became the Mayor of the Jewish Town. He had the cemetery enlarged and built a Talmudic school, a house of prayer and a ritual bath near-by. He also participated in the construction of the Jewish Town Hall, the High Synagogue ②, and his privated synagogue ⑤, set up a hospital, a poorhouse, and had all the streets of the ghetto paved. Most of these structures were concentrated in the centre of the Jewish Town, which was thus architectonicly completed and received a consistent urban plan for its future development.

In the 1620's many houses were built on the western and north-east periphery of the Jewish Town, together with the Gypsy (1613) and High-Court Synagogues (1627). The ever-increasing taxes set at the Country's Assembly in 1638, the epidemy of plague in the ghetto in 1639 and the interruption of trade as a consequence of the Thirty Years's War, brought the Jewish community in Prague to the verge of exhaustion resulting in a considerable decrease in population. Yet after the end of the war the population of the ghetto increased following an influx of refugees from Poland and the Western Ukraine, expelled by the pogroms during Chmielnicki's Uprising in 1648—1649. The great plague of 1680 at which 3,500 inhabitants of the ghetto died, postponed the introduction of measures against the increase of the Jewish population in Prague. A new disaster broke out on 21st June 1689 when 318 houses and 11 synagogues were burnt down by a great fire. In spite of all the catastrophes, the population of the Prague ghetto rose to almost 12,000 by the end of the 17th century, which made the Prague Jewish community one of the biggest Jewish communities in Europe of that time. The first detailed census of population of the Jewish Town was carried out only in 1729, when 2,335 Jewish families consisting of 10,507 individual persons were recorded (except children under the age of 10). The real number of its inhabitants was probably even higher. A new catastrophe occurred in the Jewish Town under Maria Theresa in 1745—1748 when the Jews were banished from Prague. After their return their taxes were raised to 204,000 guldens a year and then they were being raised every five years. 190 houses and 6 synagogues fell victim of a new fire which afflicted the Jewish Town in 1754. The renovation of the town together with high taxes resulted in high insolvency of the Prague Jewish community, which lost its economic significance for a long time.

The reforms of Joseph II in the period of the Enlightenment began to create conditions for a broader participation of Jews in economic and cultural life of the society. Jewish students were allowed to attend all kinds of domestic higher schools, and restrictions concerning the Jewish enterprises in production and trade were loosened up. The oldest textile factories in Prague were established mostly by Jews. Some of them were raised to the rank of nobility for their contribution to the development of industry and trade. But they gained their civil rights only after the adoption of the first Austrian Constitution in 1848 and

# Jewish Town of Prague

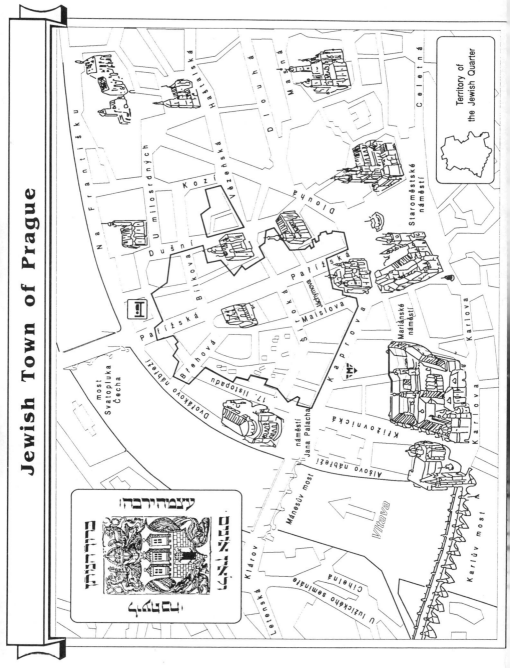

reached full emancipation only in the 1860's. In Prague it manifested itself in the incorporation of the ghetto, as Prague V - Josefov, into the covenant of the historic towns of Prague.

Better off classes moved out of the ghetto to other districts of the city after the abolition of the enforced residence in the ghetto and its gradual economic independence. The Jewish Town — Josefov had become a district of the Prague poor with unsatisfying hygienic and social conditions. That was why it was decided to rebuild the entire district following the so-called Sanitation Law of 1893. The old Prague ghetto was demolished between 1897 and 1906 and the new district was built for the most part in the first decade of the 20th century. The plan of the new district keeps approximately to the old network of streets with the exception of Pařížská Avenue, which leads across the former Jewish Town. In the newly built-up space which is a display of pseudo-historie styles and the Art Nouveau style of the turn of the 20th century, only the Old Jewish Cemetery, the Jewish Town Hall and six oldest synagogues have been preserved without change. Today these monuments form the exhibition halls of the Jewish Museum in Prague.

# Prague Synagogues

The synagogues are the most memorable monuments of the old Jewish Town. In the past they were centres of social and religious life of the community, as well as centres of education and instruction.

The oldest preserved monument of the Jewish Town and probably the oldest synagogue in Europe used until today is *the Altneuschul* (Old-New Synagogue) ①. It was built in the last quarter of the 13th century and bears witness to the significant position of the Prague Jewish community in the Middle Ages. The interior of the early Gothic two-nave space is vaulted by six fields of a five-part rib vault supperted by two octogonal pillars. Between them there is the so-called bimah with a stand for reading from the Torah, separated from the neighbouring space with a late Gothic grille. The main hall of the synagogue is enclosed on its sides with low extensions dating from the 14th up to the 18th centuries. They serve as a vestibule and women's galleries. The furnishings of the synagogue are for the most part original. Special attention should be paid to a huge banner which was given to the Prague Jewish community already under Charles IV and was restored to its present appearance in 1716. The Altneuschul is, from the time of its foundation, the main synagogue of the Prague Jewish community. Its most significant representatives worked here, e. g. Jehudah ben Bezalel called Rabbi Löw, Yom Tov Lipman Heller, Ezekiel Landau or Shlomo Judah Rapoport. Regular services take place here virtually without interruption for more than 700 years.

*The Pinkas Synagogue* ⑥ is recorded already at the end of the 15th century as a private house of prayer of the Horowitz family which belonged to the most prominent families of the ghetto. Aaron Meshullam Horowitz built the representative building of the synagogue on the site of an older house of prayer between 1519 and 1535. The high one-nave space of the synagogue is vaulted by a late Gothic reticulated vault, but there is a number of Renaissance motifs in the stone-cutting and painted decorations. In 1607—1625 the construction was extended with an aisle and a women's gallery on its southern side. After World War II the synagogue was reconstructed and converted into a Memorial to the 77,297 victims of the Holocaust from the Czech lands. In 1968 it was closed down for a new reconstruction. At that time an old ritual bath — mikvah was uncovered, together with the remains of several wells bearing witness to an old settlement in this area. At present the reconstruction of the Memorial is being finished, so it may be used again as a pious place of commemorative gatherings of the Prague Jewish community.

*The Jewish Town Hall* ② became a symbol of the autonomy of the Jewish Town in the second half of the 16th century. It was built at the cost of the Mayor of the Jewish Town Mordecai Maisel (1528—1601) by an Italian architect Pancratius Roder. The Jewish community obtained a special privilege from Ferdinand III in 1648 for their assistance in the defence of the Old Town against the Swedes — they were allowed to build a little tower with a bell on the top of the Town Hall. The Town Hall burnt down during a great fire in 1689 and was restored by a Prague baroque master builder Pavel Ignác Bayer. It burnt down again in 1754 and was renovated to its present appearance by a master builder Josef Schlesinger in 1763—1765. The new bell and tower clock date also from this time, as well as the clock with a Hebrew dial in the northern gable of the building, running backwards, which is driven by an intricate gear of a machine made in the workshop of Sebastian Laudensperger, a royal clockmaker of Prague. The Town Hall was extended in 1908—1909 with a massive southern structure and a vestibule, with a festival hall on the ground floor (today a ritual restaurant), and a conference hall on the 3rd floor. Today, just as many centuries ago, the Jewish Town Hall is the seat of all the important institutions of the Jewish community and the place of all cultural and religion events and celebrations of the Jewish holidays.

Both memorable buildings of the Renaissance ghetto are also connected with the name of the Mayor Mordecai Maisel. *The High Synagogue* ② was built probably at the same time as the Jewish Town Hall, to which it is related by its architecture and function. The High Synagogue is, contrary to custom, situated on the first floor. Originally it was accessible directly from the Town Hall and was used as a gathering place of the Council of Elders and for the sessions of the rabbinical court. Its unusually light and distinctly articulated space with a high vault and Renaissance stucco decoration differs from domestic building tradition. It

# Prague Synagogues

was also built by the master builder Pancratius Roder, who finished its construction in 1568. During the restoration of the synagogue, damaged by the fire of the ghetto in 1689 a new stone polychromic Torah ark was built in. After World War II the services in the High Synagogue were resumed for a short time. Today there is a permanent exhibition of synagogue textiles from the Jewish communities in Bohemia and Moravia there.

In 1590 Mordecai Maisel bought a piece of land on the southern periphery of the ghetto for the construction of his private synagogue. In the following year he obtained an imperial privilege for this building and in 1592 the synagogue was dedicated, on the occasion of the holiday Simhat Torah (Joy of the Torah). *The Maisel Synagogue* ⑤ was built according to a project of the master builder Judah Tsoref de Herz. At the time it was the biggest synagogue of the Jewish Town. Mordecai Maisel and his wife Frumet donated many synagogue curtains and Torah mantles to the synagogue. A Maisel banner was also kept here, which was made following an imperial privilege from 1592. The Maisel Synagogue burnt down during the fire of 1689 and was rebuilt on a smaller scale. It was restored to its present neo-Gothic appearance in 1892—1905 by the architect Alfred Grotte. Since 1965 there has been an exhibition of synagogue silver from Bohemian and Moravian synagogues here.

*The Klausen Synagogue* ④ arose on the spot of three small buildings called Klausen, destroyed by the fire of 1689 — a Talmudic school, a synagogue and a ritual bath. They were built by Mordecai Maisel on the north-east side of the cemetery towards the end of the 16th century. The new building was finished in 1694 and in 1696 it was furnished with a new three-part Torah ark, made at the cost of Samuel Oppenheim. A huge square bimah would originally stand in the middle of the nave and the seats were placed along its perimeter, as we see it today in the Altneuschul. The Klaus Synagogue was the second most important house of prayer used by the Prague Jewish community. Many outstanding rabbis worked here, such as Baruch Yeiteles, Eliezer Fleckeles, Samuel Kauder, Ephraim Teweles and others. The synagogue also served as a house of prayer and an election room of the Burial Society of Prague. Services took place here until World War II. In 1946 there was opened exhibition of the Jewish Museum, devoted to Jewish religious customs and rituals. Since 1984 there has been a permanent exhibition of Hebrew manuscripts and prints here. Temporary exhibitions of the Jewish Museum take place in the women's gallery.

A small district of Jewish houses around *the Old Schul* (7) was situated a bit further from the centre of the Jewish Town and was separated from it by the parish of the Holy Ghost. The Old Schul is, according to tradition, considered the oldest synagogue of the ghetto. Already in 1837 there was a reform service there. As the old building was not sufficient for the growing congregation, it was pulled down in 1867. In the following years there was a new synagogue built in its place, in the Moorish style, according to a project of the architects V. I. Ullmann and J. Niklas. Remarkable interior decoration of the synagogue consisting of arabesques of stylized Islamic motifs, which was made in 1882—1893 according to the designs of the architects A. Baum and B. Münzberger, gave a new name to the building — *the Spanish Synagogue* (7). In 1982 the synagogue was closed down because it was necessary to replace electric installations there. After a complete reconstruction it will be used for ritual and cultural purposes of the Prague Jewish community.

When the "Renewal Plan" for the Jewish Town of Prague was approved of, there arose the Association for the Construction of a New Synagogue in 1898. The new synagogue was supposed to be a substitution for the Gypsy, High-Court and New Synagogues, which were demolished at that time. At the cost of the Association there was built *the Jubilee Synagogue* in Jeruzalémská Street in the New Town (not far from the Wenceslas Square) according to a project of W. Stiassný by the master builder Alois Richter in 1905—1906. A great part of the original inhabitants of Josefov lived there already at that time. The painting decoration of the synagogue, marked by the Art Nouveau ornamentalism, was designed by F. Fröhlich. This synagogue is used until today for the services of the Prague Jewish community.

During the Nazi occupation public services were prohibited in 1941, all synagogues were closed down and converted to stores of confiscated Jewish property. From October 1941 to

# Prague Synagogues

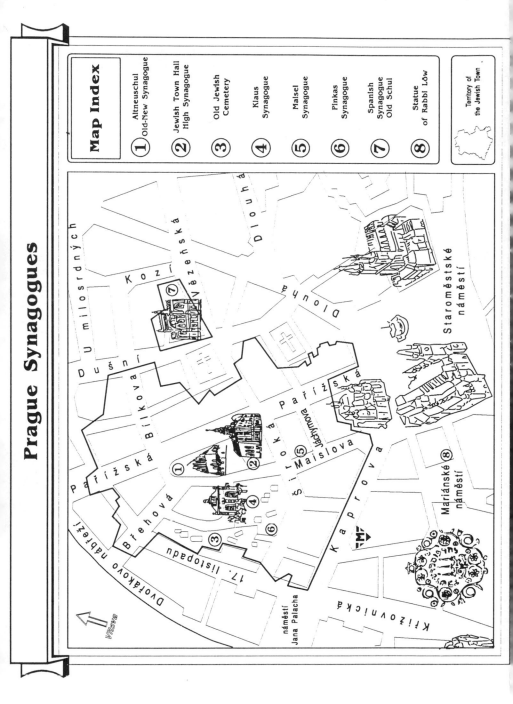

## Map Index

(1) Altneuschul
    Old-New Synagogue

(2) Jewish Town Hall
    High Synagogue

(3) Old Jewish
    Cemetery

(4) Klaus
    Synagogue

(5) Maisel
    Synagogue

(6) Pinkas
    Synagogue

(7) Spanish
    Synagogue
    Old Schul

(8) Statue
    of Rabbi Löw

Territory of
the Jewish Town

March 1945 more than 40,000 Jewish citizens from Prague and its environs were deported to Terezín ghetto and from there to other concentration and extermination camps. Only a slight number of these people returned. That was why services were resumed only in the Altneus-chul and in the Jubilee Synagogue after the end of the war. The remaining five synagogues of the former Jewish Town were turned over to the Jewish Museum which gradually opened permanent exhibitions of its collections and takes care of their preservation until today.

# The Old Jewish Cemetery

The Old Jewish Cemetery is, together with the Altneuschul, the most important monument of the Prague ghetto and one of the oldest preserved Jewish cemeteries in Central Europe.

The oldest Jewish cemetery in Prague was situated in the Lesser Town settlement round the Castle, probably in the district Újezd. The second oldest Prague Jewish cemetery was established in the 12th or 13th century on the territory of today's New Town and was abolished under Vladislav II in 1478. The remains of the tombstones from the 14th century, found during excavations on the site of the New Town cemetery, were brought over to the Old Jewish Cemetery in 1866 and embedded in the wall near the eastern façade of the Klausen Synagogue ③.

Today's Old Jewish Cemetery was founded at the beginning of the 15th century. Although it was gradually enlarged, its space was never large enough for the needs of the Prague Jewish community. As religious law does not allow the old burials to be removed, the cemetery ground had to be covered with new layers of earth. Thus a few layers of graves were formed in some places, and tombstones from different times were densely accumulated on the surface. It has created the unique appearance of this cemetery.

There are almost 12,000 tombstones in the cemetery at present. They were erected here between 1439 and 1787.

There were more tombstones set up in the Old Jewish Cemetery in the past, but many of them sank into the ground in the course of time and many others, especially those made of wood, disappeared. The historical value of the cemetery consists in the inscriptions on the tombstones, which represent an important source for the historical development of the Prague Jewish community, and in the cultural and historical significance of some outstanding personalities that were buried here. The cemetery is, at the same time, a unique art-historic monument and a witness to the development of Jewish sepulchral art.

The oldest tombstones from the 15th and 16th centuries have the shape of big black rectangular sandstone tablets with inscriptions deeply engraved in stone. Among the tombstones of this type there is e.g. that of the Prague rabbi and poet Avigdor Kara ⑦ (died in 1439) or that of Aaron Meschullam Horowitz ④ (about 1470—1545), who belonged to the foremost personalities of the Jewish Town of his time. Also the owner of the first Prague Hebrew press, Mordecai Kohen, is buried here ⑨ (died in 1592) together with his son Bezalel (died in 1589).

Only at the end of the 16th century white and red-and-brown Slivenec marble began to be used, together with plastic inscriptions in relief and various decorative elements. At the turn of the 17th century a comprehensive system of architectonic articulation of the tombstone was gradually worked out. We can trace its development in different variants up to 1787.

At the very beginning of the 17th century there appears a completely different type of the tombstone, shaped as a four-sided little house ("ohel"-tent, which was erected only over the graves of the most significant personalities. At present there are more than twenty tombstones of this kind in the cemetery.

The oldest tombstones of this kind can be found over the graves of the main representatives of the Prague ghetto in the period of the Renaissance, such as the Mayor of the Jewish Town Mordecai Maisel ⑭ (1528—1601) and Jehudah ben Bezalel, called Rabbi Löw ⑮ (1512—1609). The latter worked in Prague for 36 years as a director of the Talmudic school and as chief rabbi and published here most of his philosophical-religious writings. David Gans ⑧ (1541—1613) was a pupil of Rabbi Löw and the first modern Jewish historiographer and astronomer who met Tycho de Brahe and Johannes Kepler at the court of Rudolph II. In his chronicle called "Zemach David" (David's Offspring) he described also contemporary events from the Czech history and from the history of the Jewish Town of Prague. Joseph Delmedigo of Candia ㉒ (1591—1655) also ranked among significant scholars. He was a philosopher, physician, physicist and astronomer, who studied at the university of Padua where Galileo Galilei was his teacher. Among the latest tombstones in the cemetery there is the tombstone of the Chief Rabbi of Prague and Bohemia David Oppenheim ⑫ (1664—1736), a mathematician and a Talmud scholar who owned the biggest collection of

# The Old Jewish Cemetery

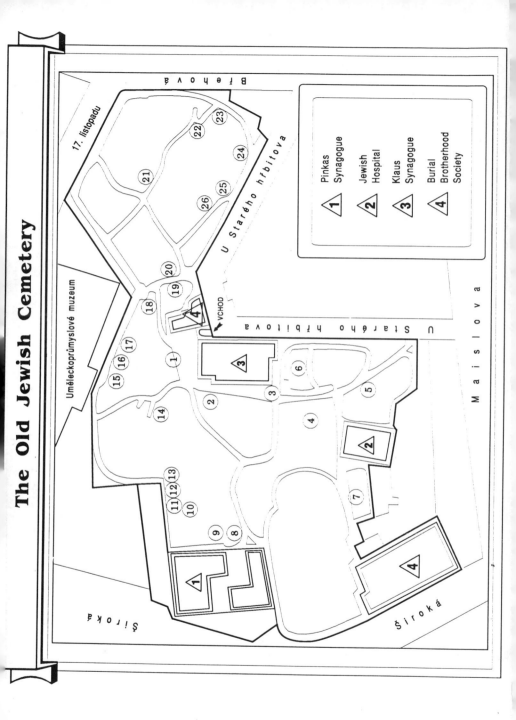

# Tombstones of Significant Personalities

(1) Beer Teller
1678
physician
Jehuda Löw Teller
1697
physician

(2) Salomon Gumperts
1729
physician

(3) Fragments of tombstones
from the 14th century, brought
over from the 'Jewish Garden'
in Vladislavova Street
in 1866

(4) Aaron Meshullam Horowitz
1545
master-builder
of the Pinkas Synagogue

(5) Moses Lipman Beck
1787
latest tombstone in the cemetery

(6) Hill 'Nefele'
children's cemetery
memorial tombstone from 1903

(7) Rabbi Avigdor Kara
1439
chief rabbi of Prague

(8) David Gans
1613
astronomer, mathematician,
historian

(9) Mordecai Cohen
1592
printer
son of Gershom Cohen,
founder of the Prague
Hebrew press

(10) Rabbi Mayer Fischel
1769
head / rector /
of the rabbinical school
in Prague

(11) Rabbi Zeev Auerbach
1632
chief rabbi of Prague

(12) Rabbi David Oppenheim
1736
chief rabbi of Prague
and Bohemia

(13) Rabbi Samuel Lichtenstadt
1752
rabbi of the Klaus
Synagogue

(14) Mordecai Maisel
1601
Mayor and Patron
of the Jewish Town
of Prague

(15) Rabbi Jehudah ben Bezalel
called Rabbi Löw or
MAHARAL of Prague
1609
chief rabbi of Prague
head of the Prague yeshivah-
a rabbinical school
his wife Perl
1610

(16) Rabbi Samuel Bezalel
1655
grandson of Rabbi Löw

(17) Rabbi Shlomo Ephraim Luntshits
1619
chief rabbi of Prague,
pupil of Rabbi Löw

(18) Hendl Bashewi
1628
wife of Jacob Bashewi

(19) Rabbi Aaron Simon Spira
1679
chief rabbi of Prague

Simon Frankl Spira
1745
Mayor of the Prague
Jewish community

(20) Rabbi Wolf Spira
1715
country's rabbi

(21) Zeew Löb
1712
pharmacist

(22) Joseph Shlomo Delmedigo
1655
mathematician, physicist,
philosopher, natural historian

(23) Rabbi Elias Spira
1712

(24) Rabbi Simon Backofen
1714

Ezriel Bondy
1716
Mayor of the Prague
Jewish community

(25) Benjamin Mayer Preslitz
1721
head of the country's
Jewish community

(26) Abraham Lichtenstadt
1702
head of the country's
Jewish community

# The Old Jewish Cemetery

old Hebrew manuscripts and prints in Prague, which is kept today in the Bodleian Library at Oxford.

From the end of the 16th century the Prague tombstones began to be decorated with various symbols, depicting usually the origin, name or profession of the deceased. Blessing hands and ewers signify the tombstones of the descendants of the biblical priestly clans Cohen and Levi. Reliefs of animals symbolize for the most part the names of the deceased. Most often we can find a lion (Jehudah, Arie, Leb), a hart (Zvi, Hirsch), a fish (Carp, Fischel), a bear (Dov, Beer), a wolf (Zeev, Wolf), a fox (Fuchs), a mouse (Meisl), a pole-cat (Iltis), a cock (Hahn), a goose (Gans) or a bird (Feigl). The professions are most commonly symbolized by instruments used in certain professions — a pair of scissors, a mortar, a lancet, a violin or a book. Figural motifs, which can be found on some tombstones, are a speciality of the Old Jewish Cemetery.

Burials in the Old Jewish Cemetery ceased in 1787 in accordance with an order issued by Joseph II prohibiting the use of burial places within the town districts. Then the plague cemetery in Olšany (today's Fibichova Street) became the chief cemetery of the Prague Jewish community for another one hundred years. Until 1890, 37,000 burials took place there. We can find there the tombs of outstanding personalities, e. g. Prague Chief Rabbi Ezekiel Landau (1713—1793), his pupil, Rabbi Eleazar Fleckeles (1754—1826), Chief Rabbi Shlomo Jehudah Rapoport (1790—1867), the reformer of pedagogy Peter Beer (1755—1838), the professors of the Prague University E. Altschul (1797—1865) and W. Wesely (1802—1870), and also of the first Prague entrepreneurs M. Jeruzalém (1762—1824), A. B. Přibram (1781—1852), Leopold Lämel (1790—1867) or Porges of Portheim (1781—1810).

The tombstones occupied all the space of the cemetery very soon and therefore *the New Jewish Cemetery* in Olšany had to be set up in 1890 (on the metro line A, station Želivského) which is used by the Prague Jewish community until today. Among the tombstones erected here between 1890 and 1940 we can find a number of neo-Gothic, Art Nouveau or modern tombstones, often made according to the designs of outstanding sculptors and architects. Among the significant personalities buried here are the Prague rabbis Dr. Nathan Ehrenfeld (1843—1912) and Dr. Gustav Sicher (1880—1960), the painter Max Horb (1882—1907), the representative of the Czech-Jewish movement Bohumil Bondy (1832—1907), the poet Jiří Orten (1919—1941) or the writer Ota Pavel (1930—1973). But the greatest number of visitors come to see the tombstone of the writer Franz Kafka (1883—1924), whose life is inseparable from the modern history of the Jewish Town and Prague.

*Arno Pařík*

# EDUARD PETIŠKA

# GOLEM

Translated by
Jana Švábová
Designed by
Vladimír Hubl
Afterwood by
Arno Pařík
Maps by René Staněk
Published by
the Publishing House
„Martin"
Printed by
G print, Ltd. Prague, Czech republic